Malcolm Gerloch was born in 1939, in Hull, East Yorkshire. He was educated at Hymers College there, and subsequently at Imperial College in London where he spent six years working for his bachelor and first doctorate degrees. After two years in post-doctoral research in magnetochemistry and ligand-field theory at the University of Manchester, he was appointed lecturer before moving, the following year, to University College, London. After three years, he was appointed to a post as Assistant Director of Research in chemistry in the University of Cambridge. He was awarded the degree of Doctor of Science there in 1980 and promoted to Reader in Inorganic Chemistry in 1984. He retired in 1999 and is an Emeritus Fellow of Trinity Hall. He and his wife, Gwyneth, now live in Canberra, Australia where they enjoy many of the usual pleasures of what might have been expected to be a quiet life in retirement. At seventy-eight,

Malcolm began writing non-scientific books to add to his four technical books and over 120 research papers. He currently boasts some dozen children's books, together with a collection of short stories and a couple of autobiographical accounts of life before and after retirement; he has recently completed his first novel. Malcolm has two daughters, three grandsons and innumerable stray cats.

Such a Silly Mistake

Malcolm Gerloch

Such a Silly Mistake

Vanguard Press

VANGUARD PAPERBACK

© Copyright 2023
Malcolm Gerloch

The right of Malcolm Gerloch to be identified as author of
this work has been asserted by him in accordance with the
Copyright, Designs and Patents Act 1988.

All Rights Reserved

No reproduction, copy or transmission of this publication
may be made without written permission.
No paragraph of this publication may be reproduced,
copied or transmitted save with the written permission of the publisher, or
in accordance with the provisions
of the Copyright Act 1956 (as amended).

Any person who commits any unauthorised act in relation to
this publication may be liable to criminal
prosecution and civil claims for damages.

A CIP catalogue record for this title is
available from the British Library.

ISBN 978-1-80016-532-8

*Vanguard Press is an imprint of
Pegasus Elliot Mackenzie Publishers Ltd.*
www.pegasuspublishers.com

First Published in 2023

**Vanguard Press
Sheraton House Castle Park
Cambridge England**

Printed & Bound in Great Britain

It is an honour to dedicate this book to the memory of my research supervisor, the man who "rescued" me as an undergraduate at Imperial College, and who later became the closest of friends:

Sir Ronald Mason, KCB, FRS.

Not for a second did he allow his considerable achievements to blind him to his roots, nor to deafen him to his friends

As always, I thank my wife, Gwyneth, for her careful proofreading and sensible advice throughout the writing of this book. I also wish to acknowledge the caring advice of two marvellous friends, Maria Altman and Edith Richie.

A Note before We Begin

For the most part, the persons described in this tale have been correctly named. Where they are not is either down to my lousy memory or to discretion. The events are more or less correctly reported but occasionally have been shifted in time to help the narrative. If you are an academic yourself, you will recognise many of my feelings and assertions; if not, I hope my story gives you an insight into the life of a don; by that, remember that I refer to *this* don. And by the way, I would hate you to think that I spent all my time flitting around the world — or Continental Europe in the present tale — for I really did do quite a lot of hard work at home in between! And when I work, I work fast. Let's not get too heavy about it all, please.

Before

1

'Jack! Who do you know in Germany who might invite me to give a talk?'

At that stage in my life, I had been an academic chemist for some fifteen years, if you count my time working for my PhD. My career had gone well for me as I moved from Imperial College, London to lectureships in Manchester University and then in University College, London; I'd had more than my fair share of luck in that I had now become an assistant director of research in the Department of Chemistry in the University of Cambridge as well as coming to hold a Fellowship in one of the colleges of that august institution. Jack Lewis was my friend and chief as professor of inorganic chemistry in Cambridge.

The position as ADR was roughly the equivalent of a university lecturer, but within the chemistry department of those days, could be held with what today would be considered to be a disproportionate bias towards research. And research was what I lived and breathed for. In fairness, I quite enjoyed lecturing, especially in topics I understood, and had no more than a useful fear of standing before a class.

Enough fear to keep me sharp. Most of my time, however, was spent trying to understand things which had never been understood before, or sometimes those which had been improperly understood. My area of research was, generally speaking, in quantum chemistry and I would hazard the guess, dear reader, that your knowledge of, and interest in, my wonderful pursuit is likely bugger all. Please be assured that this book is not intended to be an instruction manual on magnetism, ligand-field theory, quantum chemistry or even science as a whole. I promise to keep any mention of these topics to an absolute minimum. So please relax and enjoy yourself.

A researcher's lot is to read books and articles, to think and argue, to design and perform experiments where that is possible, and at all costs, to begin to understand and to make progress. The way in which research is carried out varies with the subject and with the individual. Nobody has written any rules. You make up your own. You are your own judge and jury — at least in the first instance — and your success is measured by the responses you evince from your peers. And of course, from your seniors, but why spoil such an idyll?

Consider the way the PhD work of a student in history could go. Typically, there might be several early meetings between student and research supervisor to nut out an area of research which might catch the student's imagination, and which is simultaneously deemed worthy by her boss. Another way of understanding "worthy" might be as something that, in due course, an external examiner — who would be someone like her boss — could take seriously. Then, the supervisor could suggest an area of reading and material which might yield information and ideas to an inquisitive mind. Thereafter, contacts between student and supervisor might typically be sparse. It is the *student's* PhD, after all; the supervisor has, in all probability, already got his doctorate. This whimsy summary of an arts' research programme is to be contrasted with graduate work in the sciences. To be fair, however, there has always seemed something especially honest to me, maybe brutally honest, about the way the arts chaps set about this business.

Contrast this with how a research student in physics might work for his doctorate. He would have chosen, no doubt, a supervisor in a field that particularly appealed to him. It has to be said, however, that in all subjects, students might find themselves with little or no choice if only because of the exigencies of finding suitable financial support. Anyway, the physics supervisor would probably suggest a research area which would fit nicely into his or her research area, perhaps with the idea of filling in some gap in the area or of clarifying some detail. In any case, it would surely be research into something the supervisor could advise about. Once more, after an initial start-up phase, the student would be expected to get on with it independently to some extent. Of course, the project might involve performing experiments with apparatus or theory which had been developed in the supervisor's laboratory and several other people might be involved in that enterprise. In that case, it would be inevitable that a high degree of collaboration was necessary. So a physics PhD project might well involve collaboration between student and supervisor. The individual contributions made by our fresh research student would make themselves apparent in due course and the contents of his PhD thesis would emerge as the group work progressed. The picture thus emerges — admittedly a crude simplification with some extraordinary exceptions, as where a PhD student branches out on her own and is rewarded with a Nobel Prize years later for her efforts — that research work in the sciences, especially in the experimental sciences, typically contains rather more group activity than in the arts.

This difference is even more sharp when we consider chemistry. In many areas of this subject, research is a totally collaborative affair within the supervisor's group. Projects are often shared out amongst the group members, albeit with demarcations relating to particular chemical compounds, for example, and many research publications carry long authorship banners. I have been told recently that a chemistry doctorate is nowadays little more than a research qualification for post-doctoral work. It is as if individual enquiry, individual stamp, into some area, is now made only after a research chemist leaves the nest, so to speak, and swims on his, or her, own. Personally, I had first come to believe that proposition, by the way, even in 1970. Anyway, that's enough of all this. After all, things change all the time. That's true of all human endeavour so rather than wail about how things are changing (a subject which has itself been explored in many a doctoral thesis), let's just admit that "fings ain't wot they used to be".

In the days of this story, research was undertaken in my group by a collective of individuals all working within an umbrella defined by the boss; namely me. The way I ran my research group, however, was my own, for I rarely used my office in the department, preferring instead to take a desk in the same room occupied by my post-graduate and post-doctoral students. Informal discussions and arguments might spring up at any time and would be guaranteed during coffee and tea breaks, mid-morning and -afternoon. I ran a family, in effect, in which only intensely personal matters were off-limits to the group. If I wanted to write or to think intensively, I would go off to my room in college and work alone without fear of interruption. Maybe my protégés were only too happy to get a few hours' peace.

I was only too well aware of what a privilege it was to have such a bolthole, by the way; one of many advantages conferred upon an academic's life in Cambridge.

I lived for my interactions with my research students. If you are somewhat unknowledgeable about the academic scene, my affection for my group may seem all too natural. It was, however, not universal within the chemistry departments in which I had worked, at least to the degree I practised. Some of my colleagues undoubtedly thought me naïve or gauche in this regard; others, perhaps, that I lacked confidence to maintain a proper distance. I assure you that I was as unconcerned with such views as I was aware of them. My closeness to, and affection for, my people has made my life as fulfilled as just about anything else I can imagine. I would like to think that I was a "natural" supervisor. I know that my research was also very well-regarded. Forgive the hubris but I am confident that I occupied a high position in world esteem in my field. I must immediately add, of course, that mine was a minority sport, in the land of the blind, the one-eyed man is king.

It is wonderful to be your own boss, especially without the responsibility to make your business financially viable. Academic tenure is what that is about. Again, things might be somewhat different these days but in the twentieth century, once you achieved a certain seniority, a position senior to that of a post-doctoral fellow, and maybe, to an assistant lecturer, you achieved tenure. You couldn't be sacked — not even for having an affair with your professor's daughter. Maybe not even for an affair with your professor's son. It really came down to a definition of gross moral turpitude. An affair with a vice chancellor's child might just qualify. Jokes aside, that tenure was a very real thing and there are plenty of examples of academics who sit on lectureships, doing no more than a bare minimum of work and making no contribution to the advancement of knowledge, year on year. Appealing though it was to saddle such layabouts with the least popular of duties, such retribution might often do harm to the undergraduate members of a university, so "punishments" were few and far between. No one with any sense of pride in his work, no one with an unstoppable desire to communicate his knowledge, would exploit his tenure so shamelessly, of course, but I confess that even in academe, deadheads are to be found.

Having that tenure, however, meant that you could pursue any line of research you thought fit. As a postgraduate, you had to follow directions from your supervisor — unless you were strong and able enough to challenge such advice. A post-doctoral fellow doesn't have tenure, but he might have the freedom to follow his own nose, although he may prefer to throw in his lot with the work of others, but if so, that choice is likely to be his. For that matter, there is no impediment against a tenured person choosing to pool resources with a colleague, but such would be her choice. Of course, if you need financial support — for an assistant who requires a salary, for example, or for an expensive piece of equipment — you will need to apply to one or more of various governmental, or possibly business, granting bodies. In that case, you will need to convince someone else of the value of your intended work. That can, on occasion, be a soul-destroying pursuit.

The problem of going it alone, of course, is that, as your own judge and jury, only you can decide whether to turn left or right; or, indeed, whether to admit defeat and begin again. Research can be a lonely business; sometimes frightening. Another aspect to fundamental research is worth a mention. It is that, in some respects, you become a perpetual amateur. Certainly, experience improves the *way* you tackle new problems but once you have solved one riddle, you move on. Generally, polishing your grip on one area only serves to hold you back from the fundamental. The contrast with the finely honed skill of the specialist artisan could not be starker. The best way to keep your feet on the ground is to communicate your work to others, in particular to others who can really understand it. The most immediate way of doing that is to write reports of your work — so-called research papers.

Apart from some quirky and occasionally annoying petty rules insisted upon by the editors of learned journals in which you seek to publish your work, there are no significant rules about how you go about it. If you are too long-winded, a referee or editor might tell you to cut your stuff down. In my experience, these good people are usually right, for an overly verbose presentation will only serve to put people off reading about your hard-earned research effort. Even so, learning how far you could go, what not to do and why, are all part of the business of learning how to be a good researcher. And of course, on many occasions, I could be heard berating referees and editors behind their backs. To be sure, I was not alone in that.

The other way of disseminating the fruits of your tenured labour, of course, is to give research lectures. Sometimes these take place within the structure of a conference, either by invitation or, if you are still not too well known, by submission of your topic. Yet another way, much favoured by me, is to set up a lecture tour. This often involves inviting yourself to say your piece in one after another of several venues within a geographical loop. The present story begins at such a point.

I had been invited by an Italian chemist called Dante Gatteschi to talk about my latest work in Florence. I had already met Dante, who worked in a similar field to mine. Indeed, he had only recently been hosted by me in Cambridge; as had his boss, Luigi Sacconi, on a separate occasion. I remember, by the way, delivering Sacconi to his hotel in Cambridge and while chatting inconsequentially, mentioned to him that I had recently purchased an Alfa

Romeo. I was very proud of my example of these (at that time) rust buckets.

'Ah!' exclaimed the professor, 'You show them the powder!'

At least Sacconi's English was streets ahead of my Italian. He was trying to capture our phrase about "not being seen for dust".

Anyway, there it was, out of the blue, an invitation for me to talk about my research in Florence. I'd been to Italy once before — to a conference in Rome while engaged on my doctorate work — but that was many years earlier. The chance to visit the Uffizi gallery in Florence was a great draw for me too. So I accepted the invitation and began thinking of one or two other places I might give a talk to spread the word and simultaneously learn a little more about Europe. My nose had been firmly pressed to the grindstone for years and I recognised only too well how much I needed to broaden my horizons. It might be a lovely idea to think that university dons are somehow all polymaths, knowing something, at least, about virtually everything. Well so it might, but it ain't so. I had had to work very hard to come to grips with the technicalities of my subject and had precious little time to broaden my literary, historical or artistic horizons. Like many of my colleagues, as I only later realised however, I assumed that my ignorance was unusual, was something to hide. In truth, most dons' horizons are rather limited. And most dons' eminence within their own field is only a little beyond some group average. Sure enough, there are geniuses around — certainly in places like Cambridge — but they do little to define an average. It took me quite some time after first joining that famous institution to appreciate an important, human truth, *learn to live with yourself*. I like to joke that, 'Of course I regularly read cultural books outside of my own subject; at least one a decade, whether I need to or not!' My well-read wife, Gwyneth, regularly chides me on that subject. Anyway, I was only too pleased to be able to set up another little lecture tour for myself.

I thought I'd begin my trip with another visit to Paris, once more to see Irene who had spent six months with me in Cambridge, six months of her very long stint as a PhD student at the *Université de Paris, Sud*. Now hers is an interesting story. It was while lecturing at UEA, the University of East Anglia in Norwich, at the invitation of Sidney Kettle, that I was introduced to a French researcher by the name of Olivier Kahn. I mention all these names merely to show how the interwoven network of academics works within both national and international spheres. Anyway, the point here is that Olivier had a student in Paris who wanted to include in her synthetic chemistry research, a more theoretical section, which happened to be in my area. Would I be willing to take this lady on in this rather unusual role and teach her a thing or two about my speciality? Paris would pay all necessary expenses.

I agreed, and in due course, Irene appeared in Cambridge. She was a most elegant lady, some number of years senior to my other students for the simple reason that her long PhD endeavours (twelve years, in the end) were down to her simultaneously raising a family of two children with her non-academic, medico husband, Bernard. Irene fitted into my group very well and it gave me considerable pleasure to see the envious looks of some of my colleagues who couldn't understand how I had collared so beautiful a research student. Irene's husband was a GP, I think, in Paris, and she regularly wore elegant clothes in the laboratory, so adding to the general "class" of the Gerloch group. Her feigned ignorance of the effect she was having around the place added greatly to the fun of it all. Eventually, Irene's work led to two or three significant research papers which pleased her and me alike.

My reason for telling this tale is all about Irene's PhD *viva* examination. Most of her work was in the synthetic area, as I have said. I was invited to join her PhD jury, as I learned that they call it in France, to take care of that very small part of her work which took place in Cambridge. Let me begin this tale by giving a thumbnail sketch of how PhD *viva* examinations are performed within chemistry departments in Britain.

The usual structure of these things is for an internal and an external examiner to be appointed to read the thesis and to interview the candidate. Internal, meaning someone from the same department and external, being someone usually from another institution. As like as not, these examiners are chosen, in practice, by the candidate's research supervisor. In many cases, the internal examiner might be the supervisor himself. Indeed, in some cases, the internal examiner sees his function as that of "protector" of the candidate, helping to steer awkward lines of examination into calmer waters. An external examiner with experience in these matters easily recognises what such an internal examiner is up to, and depending on how serious a matter a particular line of enquiry is, might smile and allow himself to be diverted. It is, however, always possible that the external examiner will see his line of questioning as central to the issue and therefore persist. Generally, the external examiner will try to be kind but not be a pushover.

I have been in both internal and external roles from time to time, and like anyone else in such positions, have gained confidence over the years. There was one occasion in Manchester early in my career, where I took the external examiner role. The young lady whose thesis I was examining began her defence well enough but somehow began to lose confidence as the interview progressed so that, without any prompting by me as external examiner, or by a former colleague of mine as internal, the lady began to lose it. Eventually, she was struck dumb and grew near to tears. It was all so embarrassing, especially as her work was perfectly satisfactory. I abruptly stopped the examination and told the candidate that I was satisfied with her thesis and that her job that day was just to detail some points so that I, as examiner, could be satisfied that the work was, indeed, her own. I therefore suggested that everybody take a break for a quarter of an hour, that she should leave the room to calm down, so that afterwards we could recommence the examination in the spirit of enjoyment.

To help all this along, I said, 'Before you go, I understand that you plan to do post-doctoral work in Bath (I think that's where it was). Do you know that city? Have you found a place to live?' I carried on like that for a while until she became able to string some words together again. So, on this occasion, it was the external examiner who leapt to the defence of the candidate for it is likely that few internal examiners could have done something so blatant as that. Well, having told you something of my experiences as both internal and external examiner within the British chemistry world, the following tale of my participation in Irene's jury in Paris tells a rather different story.

When I was asked to participate in Irene's doctoral jury, I had no idea what such a jury was. As I just explained, in Britain, two examiners did the trick. It turned out that there were five jurors in Paris, the most senior — the president — acted as chair during the examination, and as we shall see, as chair in the subsequent ruminations. Irene's thesis was very nearly all about aspects of synthetic chemistry, so all of my co-jurors were there to take care of those matters. The ten percent, perhaps, of Irene's work relating to ligand-field theory and magnetochemistry were for me to examine. So much was explained to me well in advance. That was some relief, for the examination was to be conducted in French, reasonably enough, and her thesis was similarly written in that language. My command of French was my best outside of my native English; it was at the level of a bare pass at O' level some twenty years earlier.

I had been sent a copy of the thesis several weeks earlier, of course. When I turned to the section relating to my expertise and began to read, I knew I was in deep trouble. Indeed, I had anticipated this and asked Irene if it really was necessary that I be a juror at all, but it was clear from her consternation that I would be letting her down badly if I refused. I was lumbered. It so happened that I and my then wife, Annette, had taken a paying guest in our large house to help defray costs. Remy was a French-speaking, Swiss, fine-arts student in the local Cambridge technical school. Annette and I, and our two young daughters, all liked Remy enormously and that was reciprocated. Remy spoke English extremely well, albeit with a very strong accent, and would often ask me about detailed nuances of meaning in English, details which many an Englishman would find perplexing. Remy, after all, regularly had to write essays in English on the subtleties of visual styles and philosophies. That would be difficult even for many a native English speaker. I was full of admiration for this foreigner's command of English.

So it was then, that when I found difficulty understanding Irene's French, I turned to Remy for help. But I had completely forgotten how unfamiliar the subject matter would be to my arts faculty friend.

'Jesus Christ!' Remy exploded as I indicated my problem.

'Sorry. Just translate what you read. Leave the understanding to me,' I said. We got by in the end, but it was an hilarious partnership that day.

Imagine then being a fly on the wall in that examination room in 1978 — actually it was a fair-sized lecture theatre — at The Sorbonne when, after some introductory remarks, the president of Irene's jury turned to me and explained that it was his honour to ask this distinguished guest from Cambridge to open the batting. I had hoped that someone else would begin the examination so that I might learn the ropes as we went along, no such luck. He added that it had been agreed that my questions and Irene's answers would be conducted in English.

The president was of slight stature, and a little portly, but exuded that confidence which only comes with years of experience and seniority. All of the French jurors wore academic dress of a pattern which appeared to me as somewhat florid, or quasi-religious even, in their style. Of course, British academic dress no doubt seems strange to foreigners too. I rather wished that I had been forewarned about dressing up — I sat there in my sombre, double-breasted grey suit — for I could have turned up in my ScD gown, a resplendent scarlet affair with shot grey silk reveres. I'd have loved to show off what Gwyneth calls my red knickers! Anyway, if Irene was nervous about her examination, I was just as nervous about my role as examiner. As was my way, however, I felt it important to put the examinee at her ease before getting down to business.

'Perhaps, Madame Morgenstern, you are a little nervous?' Irene looked puzzled. Maybe she hadn't understood my question. 'Un petit nerveux?' I continued, hoping that I had made up the correct word, or even phrase. Irene nodded, smiling a little. 'Moi aussi!' I continued. I could have said, 'Moi également!' but that was beyond my paygrade. Anyway, the humour got through and today, I like to think that I had struck an early blow for the MeToo movement. Irene and the other jury members both enjoyed the joke. A degree of calm had been achieved.

Thereafter, I asked a couple of very simple technical questions which Irene dispatched readily enough but when I stepped up the pressure — just a little — she performed less well. I was embarrassed for her and did my best to diffuse the situation before handing back to the president. It seemed to me, as I tried my best to understand some of the rest of the proceedings — a problem with the chemistry every bit as much as the language, by the way — that Irene was far more confident in the other areas and returned fire with competence.

After an hour of this, the chairman rose to his feet, followed by the rest of the jury, the candidate and thirty or so onlookers, who were colleagues, friends and family of the accused, and announced that the jury would retire to consider their verdict. Just imagine having to defend your research in front of your family! The physically small president slowly, but somewhat majestically, led the jury out of the theatre in single file and into a nearby office. It was only when all the jurors were standing, that a somewhat comical image revealed itself as the considerable physical mismatch between the jurors became evident. The man (they were all men, by the way) next to the president was as tall as his senior was short and as thin as the boss was not. Just like Laurel and Hardy, I thought. The others displayed similar variety, not so much in height but in hair colour, baldness and beards. I remembered, as a schoolkid of thirteen or so, being set the task in art class of drawing a queue of people at a bus-stop. The class had been advised to consider mixing up men, women and children; tall and short, fat and thin. I had greatly enjoyed giving a short man an enormous paunch. The art teacher had liked that, and I learned something that day.

Once out of earshot, the president let all pretences drop and there began general chit-chat about, so far as I could tell with my very limited French, nothing at all relevant to Irene's thesis. Some of the jurors lit cigarettes, others partook of water provided. After a while, copies of a form were passed around. No remarks were made about any particular aspect of the candidate's performance and I was unsure whether such might be appended later. Essentially, the form listed four possibilities — four check boxes, if you like — into which each examiner was to put his mark — fail, pass, pass with distinction, and pass with acclamation. As my piece of paper arrived, I hesitated as to whether I should tick the "pass" box or, perhaps, the "pass with distinction". As far as that part of the thesis and *viva* concerned with my speciality was concerned, I thought the candidate certainly deserved to pass but probably little more. However, most of her work was in the synthetic area, and judging by the lively discussions I had heard but imperfectly understood, to put it mildly, a notch up to "pass with distinction" might be appropriate and I felt I could wear that. Deciding to be generous, I poised my pen over the "pass with distinction" box. As my pen began to descend, the president spoke softly to another juror.

'Tell Doctor Gerloch how things are done around here.'

The juror explained, 'It is customary to pass with acclamation.'

With barely a twitch, I shifted my pen a notch to accommodate the local majority. The jury hung about for some five minutes more to give the audience the sense that some deliberation had taken place and then the president led the snake back into the lecture theatre. He immediately announced that Mrs. Morgenstern had been awarded her doctorate with acclamation. There was a whoop of delight from someone in the audience and everyone clapped thunderously.

So there it is. These things happen differently in different countries. And anyway, the main point is that Irene deserved her doctorate so why worry about charming, delightful add-ons. Since then, I learned that Irene had been appointed to a junior faculty position and had begun leading a research group of her own. In the years that followed, she has been promoted several times and has now reached the rank of professor. I am very pleased. At the time of the present story, however, she was still very new to the leadership role and had asked me if I could pop over to Paris to help her group understand an important computer program which my group and I had written over several years. I was more than happy to do this and decided to do so as the starting point for a little lecture tour on the Continent. I would spend several days in Paris helping to get my program working there and then take the train to Florence. I accepted Dante Gatteschi's invitation to give that lecture.

It was at that point when I decided to include Germany in this little tour. However, I wasn't personally acquainted with any established German chemists, within my special area or otherwise, and so I asked my boss in Cambridge, Professor Jack Lewis, a man to whom I owe a great deal. Lewis had been my boss in Manchester and then at University College in London and had asked Brian Johnson and me to follow him on his way from Manchester to Cambridge. All of that is an interesting story in itself but is hardly relevant to our present tale so I'll not muddy the waters.

'Try Rudolf Krause,' Jack suggested. I had never heard of him but readily admit that was likely my fault rather than Krause's. Apparently, Krause had been a regular visitor to University College, London during the years before Johnson's and my tenure at UCL. Jack felt sure that Krause would be happy to help me complete my little trip. 'He's a great anglophile,' he said. 'He'll do you proud.'

It turned out that Rudolf Krause was professor of inorganic chemistry at the Technical University of Braunschweig — Brunswick in its English form. I had absolutely no idea where in Germany that was. As I've indicated several times already, I was woefully ignorant of most things outside of my speciality. Anyway, I was to learn a great deal about Braunschweig, or rather of the surrounding countryside, in due course, for Krause was indeed most helpful and welcoming, offering a timeslot for my lecture, together with a couple of nights' accommodation and a small fee. That was all I wanted.

Part I

2

I had to arrange official leave from the University in Cambridge and to make sure that my absence wouldn't cause anyone undue problems. And then I was off. I flew to Paris, arriving at Charles de Gaulle airport around midday on a sunny April Tuesday in 1987. That wonderful piece of architecture was yet still rather new. It was certainly eye-opening to me, for I had long had a keen interest in art and architecture. Irene met me and drove me to a rather splendid small hotel in the Latin Quarter. She left me to find my bearings, arranging to have me picked up the following morning.

Marvellous! I had my first afternoon and evening to myself. I could re-acquaint myself with a few bits of the great metropolis and enjoy a pleasant evening meal in a city I loved. My lousy French didn't prevent my ordering what I wanted in restaurants and bistros, but I remember, with acute embarrassment, an occasion in my early twenties when I decided to try a different style of steak from entrecote or filet, ordering steak tartare *avec des petits pois*. The waiter had stared at me before deciding to say nothing. When the tartare arrived, I realised how silly I had been and was pleased to see no peas. Only after I had consumed the steak — with relish, I might add — did the waiter front up with a dish of hot peas. One should never forget that no matter how clever you may think you are, a lack of data can be paralysing; life requires experience.

I didn't give any lectures in Irene's laboratory on this occasion but rather spent my time installing my computer program and then trying to debug the damn thing when it didn't work first time. My team back in Cambridge and I sorted the problem out in due course, but my time in Paris turned out to be somewhat fraught. These things happen, unfortunately.

On my last evening there, Irene took me out to a rather posh restaurant for dinner. It was an odd sensation, I found, to be the male guest of a female host; but then, why not? No doubt her department was paying for the evening, but I still felt awkward. The waiter made an obvious assumption as he passed me the wine list. Some of the wines at the top of the list were priced at the franc equivalent of several hundred pounds; and that was in 1987. I hurriedly moved on to a more sensible price range and was taking a little time choosing when Irene uttered a little cry and hurriedly swapped her wine list with mine. The point was that this was one of those places where the hosting male is given the priced list while the female guest is given the unpriced one. I pointed out to Irene that it was quite ridiculous for her to let me choose a wine costing what I might have to wait several months to earn and I simply insisted that either she choose the wine or that she swap the lists back. It was, however, an object lesson in learning how the other half lives, in how snobbish some levels of society can be; or, if you invert the argument, how gauche I was. Mind you, my — by then — seventeen years as a Fellow of a Cambridge college had opened my eyes to a quality of living that was quite unknown to me from childhood, one more of the wonderful privileges of Cambridge college life for which I am immensely grateful.

I remember the time when it had fallen to me and one other Fellow, to audit the college's cellars. It turned out to be fun and very illuminating but something not to be done more than once in a Fellow's career, if only because of the time-consuming, and in the end, boring nature of the count. Anyway, in those days, my college's wine was housed in five different cellars under different buildings. Some of the cellars were quite small, cramped and fusty. All were cool and damp. The racks were designed to hold the maximum number of bottles within any given space. None of those arty-farty wine racks so beloved of chic kitchen magazines, racks destined to hold a dozen bottles if you're lucky. No, the college racks were a fine example of "close packing". Whether you understand that term in a technical way or simply as a tight adjectival phrase, I'm sure that you get the point. The college butler took me and my co-counter from cellar to cellar. It turned out that my colleague was rather slow at counting and it became only too clear after a short time that we'd be at it for hours, if not days, if something was not done to speed the process. It was difficult for the butler to point this out so I, the junior of the two Fellows by far, simply took charge and told my colleague to help the butler check his list while I did all the counting. The older Fellow was actually quite relieved to let me do all the work and things sped up well.

It turned out that Trinity Hall possessed at that time (1971) some fifteen thousand bottles of vintage port and a further thirty-odd thousand bottles of other wines, many with labelled vintage also. You could swim in the stuff! We had begun the audit around nine a.m., broken for an hour's lunch at twelve-thirty p.m., and completed our job by about three-thirty p.m. The butler, however, was heartbroken; devastated. Why? Because we had found eight more bottles of wine than were on his list. The butler knew where the discrepancy lay and hurried off to recount the bottles of one particular Medoc. But he returned, saying that he agreed with our count.

'Drink them!' was my immediate suggestion to the butler. Oh no! he couldn't do that. 'Why not?' I asked in ignorance at that time as a green new recruit to the Fellowship. Green, because I soon came to know what most of the Fellowship knew, that our butler was no laggard with respect to the college cellars. The point is, however, that the two or three dozen bottles which found their way down the butler's throat throughout any given year were accounted for by the utmost subtlety of butlerian accounting methods. No wonder he was upset! He must have been doing some of his accounting while partaking of his ill-gotten gains. Anyway, after three days, he beamingly announced to the auditing Fellows that he had found his mistake and the count was now correct.

'Thank God for that!' I breathed to my colleague and went about my proper business, 'Eight bottles in some forty-five thousand and then only an indifferent Medoc!'

Actually, I was rather pleased to see the butler discomforted at that time. It served as an amusing payback for an incident which had occurred some months earlier. You see, Fellows met for dinner every Monday evening. (It later became every Tuesday as the chef complained about the difficulty of getting supplies of various ingredients for his sumptuous offerings from the London markets in time. I recall that that change was agreed to unanimously by the Fellowship, of some thirty-five persons, in mere seconds.) On those occasions, the various wines offered before, during and after the meal — in quantities which seemed inexhaustible — were all free; part of what was splendidly referred to as "commons". By the way, before your hackles rise about public money being spent on such disgraceful private pursuits, let me assure you that no public financing of our private debauchery was involved at all; the money all came from private endowments made to the college over the years, correction, centuries. The same arrangements operated for the occasional, "special" dinner provided by the college. However, it was also possible to "dine in" on other days, and indeed, to bring guests. The food for the Fellow, and one guest per month, were *gratis* but all wines had to be paid for by the Fellow. I remember asking the butler how the wine accounting took place. Was someone keeping tabs on how many glasses were drunk, for example? Indeed, some colleges in both Oxford and Cambridge do work an "honour system" in which each Fellow signs a chitty for each glass consumed. Trinity Hall was having none of that, explained the butler. Instead, each Fellow was assigned to a grouping decided upon by the butler from his general observations. Apart from the occasional Fellow who was teetotal, the rest were described as "light drinkers", "medium drinkers", or "heavy drinkers".

'Which am I?' I asked, rather naively, I admit.

'Oh! You're a heavy drinker, sir,' replied the butler, with a somewhat heavy emphasis on the "sir". I thought his assessment was in order but was amazed at how quickly he had made it, considering I had only been in the place for about a month at that time. Silly me.

It seems to me at this point that I should spend a few moments in serious defence of my reputation. You will have gathered that I like my bit of fun and I am happy to share it. But I do worry now that I may have given the impression that academics in general, and I in particular, don't take our job seriously. I really must spend a little time providing some clarity here but let me say right at the beginning that I am not trying to write a serious tome on academe. Such writing has its place, but it can get very dry so please be assured that what immediately follows is to be considered as contraceptive rather than prescriptive.

It has been my pleasure, and honour frankly, to have known and worked with some incredibly talented and hard-working people — in London, in Manchester and in Cambridge where I have held teaching and research positions. The same goes for those collaborators or just acquaintances I have been associated with in many other academic institutions around the world. At the time of my retirement, I had spent twenty-nine years in Cambridge and at Trinity Hall so forgive me, please, if I focus on those years and those institutions. Let me say a few words first about the business of teaching.

Some would argue that such is the most important function of a university don, others that research is paramount. I would argue that the one informs the other. Undoubtedly, some dons are better lecturers than others. Equally, some are better researchers than others. It's no good arguing that hot-houses like Cambridge have the power to attract the very best, for the very best researchers may be far from the very best teachers. I do not wish to imply that the better one is at one, the worse the other. As in any other field of human endeavour, skills vary from person to person and from field to field. Certainly, there are some extremely clever people in the Cambridges of this world, but they are still as capable of messing something up as anyone else. Having said that, I must say that I have been amazed at the quality, the intelligence and the devotion of colleagues I have met in the place.

I have already said what a privilege it is to hold a college Fellowship in Cambridge. I had my own room in a quiet building where I could think, read and write in total peace. I well remember struggling to understand a bit of physics for a book I was writing, and I spent most hours in the week, for many weeks, reading so many physics tomes and teaching myself the subject until I was able to extract what I needed. Further, one of my colleagues, Mike Stobbs, who was a lecturer in the university and "ran" their electron microscope, college Fellow with responsibilities for physics teaching, and very dear friend, spent quite a long time teaching me some of the rudiments of his subject. That was one of the bonuses of college life, meeting daily with folk from other sciences and other faculties. Such meetings might not always be occasions to learn technically about another subject. More often, they would simply be occasions to understand others' points of view, to gain some insight into the way the other half think.

C.P. Snow, who was a personal friend (from Emmanuel College) of John Collier, one of the many law Fellows in Trinity Hall — his speciality being international law — had famously discussed his concept of "The Two Cultures", in reference to the arts and the sciences, never the twain shall meet. Well, he may not have been right. Whether he was or not, to rub shoulders daily with talented colleagues from the history faculty, or the law in all its glorious manifestations, linguistics, the sciences of a biological bent or theoretical, with mathematicians, with theologians, with a classics scholar, Colin Austin, who discovered a previously unknown play by Aristophanes, with academic medics — physicians and also a surgeon, Roy Calne, for example, who designed (if that's the right word) and performed the world's first liver transplant, with the professor of music, composer Alexander Goehr, with Peter Holland, later to become head of the Shakespeare Institute in Stratford-on-Avon, with Martin Hinds, an Arabist of some renown who became another close friend of both Gwyneth and me; to meet all these over lunch or, more leisurely, over dinner was a marvellous, mind-broadening thing.

To be a member of the college governing body which met at regular intervals to decide issues ranging teaching responsibilities, college finances and investments, the terms of contracts for various college servants, student examinations, college sports, and really anything any Fellow may wish to have considered by his peers; that was an education in itself, not least in how to take responsibility (and how, on occasion, to learn patience). At lunch for several years, I would chat daily with an Honorary Fellow and eminent educationist, Lionel Elvin, whose illustrious career had spanned being director of the Department of Education at UNESCO in Paris, director of the Institute of Education in the University of London, to being president of Ruskin College in Oxford, amongst several other remarkable achievements. He had been an accomplished athlete in his youth. He was also one of the kindest, most tolerant, most modest and amusing people I have ever known. Such is the privilege of fellowship in Cambridge and similar institutions.

Mind you, in an attempt at some balance, while I can vouch for the generosity of spirit amongst the fellowship of *my* college, an atmosphere of comradely companionship which predated my tenure by a very long time indeed, I am assured, the same is/was not the case for several other colleges from which one learned of many cat fights with causes ranging from jealousy (professional or otherwise) to downright nastiness. No names; no pack-drill, sorry. It was a lucky day for me when Trinity Hall offered me a Fellowship.

It also occurs to me that I ought to say a little about the structure of Cambridge University and its colleges. There are constituent colleges in the University of London — University College, Imperial College, King's College, for example — but these demarcations effectively only serve to separate self-contained institutions within the whole. In Manchester, you are a student or teacher at the Victoria University of Manchester and that's it. But in Oxford and Cambridge, things are quite different. Individual, autonomous colleges were founded at different times and in their own right. By that I mean that each college is sovereign, and originally anyway, can do what it likes, how it likes. Much later on (after a few centuries, that is), an over-arching structure called the University of Cambridge (or Oxford, as the case may be) was set up as a coordinating arrangement.

I only know a little about all this, I confess, but suffice to say that the university cannot tell the colleges what to do. When it comes to admitting freshmen from schools around the country (or from abroad), however, some sort of understanding has been reached. For example, the university runs the various laboratories around the place, and for quite obvious reasons of physical size, there is a limit to how many new undergraduates in chemistry, for example, can be admitted in any one year. Each college decides who will be admitted to its establishment — and each college decides such matters for itself, as a sovereign body — but between them, they had better not admit more than the chemical laboratories can house or, similarly, than a history lecture theatre can seat. Therefore, there has to be understanding between colleges and university. That is less difficult than might appear, for the individuals in the university actually making these decisions, also hold Fellowships in the various colleges. So it's really a matter of changing your hat back and forth.

The too brief summary I have given here no doubt seems endlessly confusing but after centuries of practice, the system seems to work. From a practical point of view, laboratory classes and lectures are given in university premises. Any given class of undergraduates will have members from many colleges. Students and teachers will normally lunch and dine in college. Supervisions, as they are called in Cambridge — or tutorials in Oxford and pretty well anywhere else — are usually given in college, and even if not, are organised by individual colleges. The progress of each undergraduate throughout his or her, normally three, years is carefully followed by college tutors — and ultimately, by the senior tutor — so the impersonal nature of less fortunate university courses is replaced by a close and caring watch. Furthermore, undergraduates typically see their supervisors several times a week, often in groups of two, or maybe individually. In "redbrick" institutions, undergraduates may receive just one tutorial every two weeks and then in a group of six or even ten. Such is the true advantage of being an undergraduate in one of the few older universities in Britain. Of course, all this costs money and colleges charge fees in addition to those levied by the university.

By the way, let me return briefly, and by way of some light relief, to the subject of buttling. At the beginning of each academic year, and by way of welcome, the college entertains all new undergraduates with a reasonably special dinner. On these occasions, Fellows are spread out and seated amongst the fresh-faced, post-"schoolies" (a useful Australian title, I think) rather than at "high table". The students possibly have their best meal of the year (and it's free) while the Fellows are to be satisfied with probably their plainest. Much more serious for many Fellows is the unaccustomed semi-drought so far as the accompanying wine is concerned. But duty is duty.

So there I was, surrounded by half a dozen or so young men and women, some almost too nervous to speak, others determined to tough it out and show how sophisticated they were; and Malcolm in the middle, hoping to survive. On the occasion I describe here, some seating joker had surrounded me with mostly young ladies. I wasn't going to let that phase me. I spotted the under-butler approaching us from my right. I pointed out to the young lads and lasses surrounding me that it was wine time and apologised for the fact that it would be a long wait for round two.

I turned to the girl on my left and said, 'You will have a glass of wine with your meal, won't you?' only to be surprised by her reluctance. The under-butler arrived and offered a white and a red to me. I selected the red and he charged my glass. He walked behind me and repeated his offer to that girl on my left. She put her hand flat across her glass. I was impressed. She wasn't as naïve as I had supposed, for she clearly knew how to indicate her refusal. I gently took hold of her wrist and removed her obstructing hand. 'Red' I said to the butler. He filled her glass. I took her glass and placed it next to my own. All those around, including the under-butler, were quite amused by my antics.

Much later on (it seemed an eternity to me), I caught sight of the butler approaching from my right once more, a bottle in each hand. He refilled my glass without asking and then, as he began to refill "my" second glass, enquired in somewhat exaggerated and obsequious tones, "Is the young lady still drinking, sir?" What a sophisticated put-down!

I must return now to my lecture tour.

3

I took the train from Paris to Florence. I remember eventually going through a long tunnel and finding that signs were now in Italian rather than French. In the first station we stopped at, I leaned out of the window and saw a sign which read *Sottopassaggio*. I remain as proud today as on that seminal occasion when I worked out that this meant "subway". As for the rest, it was all foreign to me. I changed trains in Milan but had no time to leave the station. It was a relatively short journey then, as I remember it anyway, before the train trundled into Firenze. Okay, so I'd also learned the Italian for Florence. The train was about thirty-five minutes late.

As I left the platform and was met by Dante Gatteschi, I apologised profusely for my late arrival, assuming that Dante had been hanging around for, maybe, an hour. Dante looked puzzled for a moment before replying, 'It is normal. I have just arrived. Only two minutes ago!' Another lesson for your hero, time runs slowly in Italy.

Dante took me to meet some of his colleagues for lunch in a small restaurant near his department. They, too, had only just arrived. My learning was confirmed. They were a lively, pleasant bunch of people, easy to get on with and happy. There was some discussion of our mutual scientific interests but not much, which suited me for I preferred to save the juicy bits for my lecture. As our party left the restaurant, the subject had got round to politics about which I had always maintained a morbid and unhealthy, though passing, interest. This was the time — not unusual, of course — when Italian governments fell with breath-taking regularity.

'Who's in power at the moment?' I asked my host.

Without pausing for breath, Dante raised and twisted his wrist as he consulted his wristwatch in reply. I thought that was a pretty sophisticated response.

Various plans had been made for my visit. I was to lecture that afternoon, after which I would be taken to my hotel. Later I would be picked up by one of Dante's research group, who would take me to join a small group in Dante's home for a pre-prandial drink, and then onto some place for dinner. I would be left to my own devices for the next day except that Dante promised to pick me up and take me for lunch in an old part of the city. I was very pleased with all that had been arranged and settled into a happy mood. My lecture went well and there were plenty of questions and a lively discussion afterwards. One of Dante's group drove me to my hotel, which turned out to be very comfortable and conveniently placed centrally in the city which I intended to explore a little next day. It was barely half an hour later that another of Dante's group arrived to convey me to the drinks party at Dante's place.

That was situated, as far as I could work out, well within Florence's boundary in, what seemed to me anyway, an old part of town. All around were stuccoed four-or-more storeyed buildings painted in the sort of colours which stand out so beautifully in the Italian sunshine — ochres, creams, burnt sienna, warm earthy tones. However, wherever I looked, I saw painted walls with either badly worn patches or sometimes with strips of paint simply peeling off everywhere. The building which turned out to be where Dante lived was no different and I assumed that this was a poorer part of town and that Dante could only afford a rather modest house. Dante's postdoc led me to the door, through which was a small vestibule, stairs and a lift.

I immediately recognised my first mistake, that Dante did not own this four-storeyed dump but only an apartment within it. We left the lift at the third floor, crossed a small passageway and rang the bell in the middle of a somewhat beaten-up high, very Italian-looking, door. Dante answered the call, greeting us with typical Italian enthusiasm, and ushered us inside. There were gathered around ten or so of Dante's research group, some, it appeared, with their wives or girlfriends, already suitably provided with a glass of something. However, by far the most remarkable sights to greet my eyes were the size of the room we were in and the quality of its decoration and furnishings. It was a double storey affair, immaculately provisioned, decorated and lit in the chicest style. I then remembered how the Italians have always stood out for their collective sense of style. The place must have cost a bomb, clearly far more than I could afford. The contrast with the outside of the building was stunning.

Later, I asked Dante about that difference and my host explained some of the complex taxation system then — and as far as I know, still — obtaining in Italy, the long and short of which is that it makes little sense to paint the outside of your apartment block. I couldn't fathom the logic then, I must say, and nor can I now. Nevertheless, here was an object lesson in not jumping to conclusions, of not judging a book by its cover.

I remember being taken out for dinner after that, but for the life of me, I cannot remember anything at all about the evening. That is most unusual for me for my memory about such matters is usually crystal clear. I guess I suffer some of the same shortcomings as everyone else.

My memory of the following day, though not sharp, is much more expansive. Dante had arranged to meet me at midday and take me for lunch; we had agreed to meet at the north end of the Ponte Vecchio, that famous old bridge — which is what that name means, by the way — as I had signalled my intention of including it in my limited itinerary. So, soon after breakfast, I made my way to the place I had most wanted to visit; indeed, in my (usual) ignorance, apart from that Old Bridge over the River Arno, the Uffizi gallery was the only place of which I knew anything in Florence.

I had long had an interest in pictures, and when a student at Imperial College, had visited the Tate gallery in London dozens of times, though the National Gallery only twice, my interests being polarised towards the more modern era. Nevertheless, the Renaissance collection of Botticelli paintings in the Uffizi, especially *The Birth of Venus*, just couldn't be missed.

I was surprised to find that I hadn't to queue for admission to the Uffizi and it didn't take me very long to find that picture. I was amazed and enraptured by its almost transparent beauty. Like the world and his wife, I had seen dozens of reproductions of Venus on her shell, but none captured the delicacy, yet intensity, of the real thing. I had been similarly surprised, years earlier in Paris, by Da Vinci's *Mona Lisa* in the Louvre. I had expected to be underwhelmed by familiarity — by how corny these images were, if you like — but instead, was overwhelmed by their quality. In the end, I spent about an hour in the Uffizi, only staring, gawping, swimming in Botticelli's pictures. An hour has always been my limit for standing in art galleries and even the giants on offer couldn't overcome that.

I filled in the next hour before meeting Dante by walking, somewhat randomly, around the streets nearby, glancing in shop windows at various offerings of Italian fashion but mostly just wallowing in the Florentine atmosphere. Such has always been my method of exploring new cities. I remember how I had learned the ropes in Copenhagen some ten years earlier. I had spent three weeks in that fine capital, learning about an experimental technique in spectroscopy — from an Australian scientist, Ray Dingle, in the Ørsted Institute — and giving a couple of lectures there.

One day, I took off for the city centre armed with a small folding map in my back pocket. My bus had dropped me off at Nørreport station. I spent three or four minutes studying my map before stuffing it back into my pocket. My intention was to consult it again only in dire emergency for I preferred to "feel" my way around a strange town, to keep an eye on the skyline and any prominent towers or spires but otherwise to make my exploration something of a random adventure. I much prefer this to deliberately seeking out particular places. On a later return visit to that city, I was sneakily pleased to guide a visiting American, a visitor who had, by that time, been in Copenhagen for nearly a year, around some of the back streets there. I confidently marched from one district to another while my map-wedded host scrabbled to memorise the route.

Well, I reached the agreed meeting place in Florence on the dot of noon. I forgot about Italian timekeeping, however. Dante hadn't appeared even after a quarter of an hour. So, I decided to make a short exploration of the Ponte and risk causing Dante to wait himself. It was a happy decision for otherwise I probably wouldn't have found the time to do it. I didn't go right across the bridge for fear of missing my host but in that brief incursion I caught an impression of the shops built into the sides of that famous crossing. Even by the time that I returned to the meeting place, there was no sign of Dante, but he turned up pretty soon after that. He made no apology for his lateness. I didn't expect one.

Dante greeted me with the idea that we should have lunch at a little place he knew on the south bank of the Arno. That way, we could see that very old church, the Basilica di Santo Spirito, from the outside at least, as well as taking in the quite magnificent view of the rest of Florence from the elevated vantage point immediately south of the river. From there, the view of the most obvious and famous of all buildings Florence had to offer, that of the Cathedral of Santa Maria del Fiore with its wonderful tiled dome, called the Duomo, was breath-takingly beautiful.

Later that afternoon, I walked around the cathedral's marble walls outside and then moved inside. I was amazed at how dark it was in there, although that might, in part, have been due to my just having left the bright light outside; but also, how plain. The contrast with the inside of St. Peter's Basilica in Rome, which I had seen some fifteen years earlier, could not have been sharper. Meanwhile, however, my lunch with Dante was a most pleasant affair and we lingered for quite some time in that little trattoria. Afterwards, Dante drove me back to the Piazza del Duomo ready for my explorations and where we said our farewells. Later, I had a little time left in the afternoon after gawping at the Duomo, so I went on one of my random walks until I found some shop windows with displays of modern Italian furniture. I was utterly entranced by the designs and very envious. Until, that is, I saw some of the price tags. Sadly, those works of art were not for me — any more than any of the paintings in the Uffizi!

Eventually, I felt the pangs of hunger once more and went in search of some place for my dinner. Tight wad, as ever, I found an inexpensive place in a side street whose menu seemed more reasonable than the furnishings I had envied earlier. As I made to open the restaurant door, a waiter held it open for me from inside.

'*Prego*!' he said and led me to a small table. The waiter held a chair for me. '*Prego!*' he repeated. As I sat down, he moved the chair in beneath me. '*Prego!*' he said again. Being the lightning-fast linguist I am, I surmised that *prego* meant just about anything from "greetings" to "voila" to "please" to "after you" to "welcome". I ordered a beer and began to peruse the menu. I could translate almost nothing, and it didn't occur to me to ask for a menu in English. What a sophisticated traveller I was! But I did see my favourite soup, *stracciatella*.

I had enjoyed this egg-drop soup for the first time during my trip to Rome several years earlier. Essentially, you whisk together eggs, parmesan cheese with a touch of nutmeg and stream the mixture into a hot broth. Probably the most common broth used worldwide is a chicken stock; and there's nothing wrong with that. But one version of the soup, which is distinctly Roman, is made with beef stock and such had been my first experience of the soup, and the second, and the third, and... A colleague from that conference and I had feverishly consumed a bowl of Roman *stracciatella* every evening of our time at that conference. So, for old times' sake, I chose the beef variant that evening in Florence. The only dish I came close to translating for a main dish — for I didn't feel like a pasta — was *pollo arrosto con peperoni* which I quite correctly understood to be roast chicken with peppers. I knew my translation was correct because that is what arrived in due course.

'*Prego!*' said the waiter as he placed the soup down in front of me. '*Prego!*' he said as he placed half a roast chicken in front of me. '*Prego!*' he said as he served me another beer. I got the idea.

I mused over the two days I had enjoyed in Florence as I slowly ate my dinner. I always eat slowly; I like to enjoy every morsel. It had been a most pleasant visit, I had cemented my relationship with Dante somewhat, and my talk had been well-received, I thought. I was happy. I slept well that evening and caught the train north at nine-thirty the following morning.

4

My journey took me almost due north when you allow for the terrain. Florence to Bologna, to Milan, to Lugano; to Basel in Switzerland; to Frankfurt in Germany, to Göttingen, and finally to Hanover where I changed onto a local train for the short journey east to Braunschweig.

I was met by a middle-sized, middle-aged man, by Rudolf Krause himself. Krause had a sallow complexion and a somewhat dour presence. He didn't smile as he greeted me but was, nevertheless, perfectly courteous. As we made our way to his car, he explained that he would take me to my hotel located in Wolfenbüttel, a small town some thirteen kilometres south of Braunschweig, leave me to my own devices for the evening, and pick me up in the morning. He explained that the hotel restaurant would provide a good meal and that all expenses would be met by the University of Braunschweig.

During the drive, he also gave me a running commentary on the names of districts, monuments, and both old and new buildings in the city as each came into view. Nothing was left out, it seemed to me, as I tried to keep up, but truth to tell, I was a little weary after my journey — though why that should be as I had been sitting most of the way, but that's the way of long journeys I suppose — and I failed to absorb much of Krause's tour guide.

Braunschweig is an old city with many splendid mediaeval buildings to be proud of. By 1987, in common with so many fine old cities, Braunschweig had thrown up many new concrete blocks of, no doubt, great ergonomic convenience, but to my mind, with little architectural or aesthetic merit. Krause's route had taken us past so many of these monstrosities that I was left with unfortunate memories of the place. As things turned out, these boring aspects of Braunschweig came to play a disproportionate role in my feelings about the place. Wolfenbüttel, on the other hand, provided me with some delightful, if quirky, memories.

Wolfenbüttel, like Braunschweig, is located in the German state of Lower Saxony bordering Schleswig Holstein to the north and Westphalia to the west. My immediate impression of Wolfenbüttel was of the profusion of timber-framed buildings; indeed, as I later discovered, Wolfenbüttel is famed for having the largest number of such structures in Germany. These lovely buildings reminded me of those in several towns and cities in England — Guildford, York, Ludlow, for example — but one could never be confused about which country one was in. The buildings in Wolfenbüttel are, by and large, at least one storey taller than such timber-framed buildings in England; sometimes two. And rather than being painted in the usual English white — although those in Suffolk would be an obvious exception, of course — they were meticulously painted in a variety of colours, yellows of different shades in particular as well as whites and creams. I was struck by how well-cared for everything was, how different from the public face in Florence. The whole place was almost prim and proper, you might say. Perhaps rather precious. Nevertheless, I felt easy and happy in that town as I took a short walk near my hotel after checking in after Krause dropped me off. Krause was right; the hotel restaurant was more than adequate, and I enjoyed my first German schnitzel that evening before retiring to a most comfortable bedroom. Yes, this was going to be a pleasant visit.

Krause himself picked me up after breakfast next morning, and as we drove into the university, provided another running commentary on the sights — buildings, railway stations, road intersections, post office buildings. I'm afraid that I switched off well before we reached our destination. After dropping off my briefcase in his office, I was taken to meet Krause's research group. Of course, both my host and I were well aware that my research area was theoretical while these students were working on synthetic chemistry projects. I use pencils, chalk and computers, while they used beakers and Bunsen burners. There is little common ground between these disciplines, but I was hopeful that members of other research groups in the department as a whole, from physical or theoretical chemistry perhaps, might find some interest in my work. Anyway, if the worst came to the worst, I reasoned, it pays to advertise.

Krause's people were pleasant enough, however, and many spoke English quite well which was a deal more than could be said of my German. They told me a little about their work over coffee and I tried hard to look interested, but their greatest curiosity was aroused about the University of Cambridge itself. I felt that I had survived the morning in reasonable shape and then it was time for my lecture. There were few questions afterwards, although there had been warm applause. I had expected little else, but you never know.

I remember a lecture I gave at Bristol University in which my honesty was, in my view at least, too forthright. I felt later that I had misjudged my audience and was unhappy afterwards. Yet, after some months, a post-graduate, Bob McMeeking, who had been in my audience, wrote to me asking for a position as a post-doctoral Fellow (post-doc in the vernacular). Bob turned out to be one of the very best colleagues that I ever had, and he remained in, then out, then in again, of my group for many years. You never can tell, it seems.

Anyway, lecture done and Krause and several of his group took me to the university canteen for lunch. It was a simple affair and wholesome enough, but I had hoped for something a bit more special. Cambridge has spoilt me, I'm afraid. After lunch, Krause took me aside and suggested that he show me the border with East Germany.

Nothing could have been further from my mind. In answer to my first question, Krause pointed out that Braunschweig was only about forty-five kilometres west of the Helmstedt-Marienborn border crossing with the East.

'Here we are in the nearest sizeable city to the border,' he said. I thought that this would be a wonderful opportunity to see the east-west German border and thanked Krause warmly for his offer.

'Fine. Let's go.' Krause did not waste words on this occasion and led me to his car. Once in it, however, he began his tour guide once more but as we approached our destination, he broke off and explained that he would like to show me the border from two different locations so that, before looking at the border crossing point itself, we would drive a few kilometres into the country to get a rather different view. In no more than a few minutes, we left behind all signs of habitation and Krause parked his car and invited me to follow him into a field.

It could have been any field in England, I thought. After a short walk, we came across a narrow, dirt track. Actually, it was just grass worn down by repeated use. It ran immediately adjacent to a wire fence.

'This is technically the true border between East and West Germany,' Krause told me.

It comprised rusty metre-high iron stakes at roughly three-metre intervals with a single strand of rusty barbed wire running along the top. It would barely have dissuaded a cow from wandering in or out.

'Is this the border?' I asked, with some incredulity.

'Wait. We'll walk a few metres further along this fence so that you can see over that little mound,' Krause replied, indicating a little hillock of green grass on the other side.

That was when I saw the true border fence for the first time. Set back into the East German side of the border wire by some twenty or more metres was The Fence. It comprised two parallel galvanised, possibly six-metre-high, chain-link fences with Y branches at the top of each, strung with coils of shiny razor wire. These two fences were some ten or more metres apart and between them, as dramatically pointed out by my host, was a V-shaped "moat" made of concrete.

'That's a tank trap,' Krause explained. 'Nobody could drive a truck at those wire fences and hope to get across. Their vehicle would break in two in that concrete gully. Of course, nobody wants to go from West to East. That fence is to keep those people on the other side, in.'

There was more. Every half-kilometre, the East German authorities (for which, read Russians, I thought) had built watchtowers. They looked somewhat like the watchtowers I had seen in so many war movies about POW and concentration camps and such. At the top of each metal tower was a sheltered deck which, Krause explained, was manned non-stop by two East German soldiers. For twenty-four hours each day.

I let my gaze wander, first to the right — roughly, that is, to the south — and then to the left/north. The border fence stretched out before me as far as I could see on that bright day, uphill and down dale, to borrow a well-worn phrase, from the Baltic to the border with Czechoslovakia. Endless. It was only on seeing that prison, close up and personal as it were, that I really began to comprehend a little of what had happened in the years immediately before and after my birth. I had seen movies, I had seen documentaries, I had read some articles. Seeing something so real, though, meant so much more. I didn't know what to say. Krause looked at me as I thought my thoughts. I couldn't speak. Krause chose not to.

Just then, seemingly out of the blue, an East German soldier appeared on the opposite side of the border wire, just a metre from we two gawping academics. The soldier, dressed in a dull mud-green uniform and carrying a rifle (or was it a semi-automatic? I wondered) hung from his shoulder, neither spoke to, nor looked at, us.

'*Guten Tag,*' said my host. The soldier made no reply and continued to look straight in front of him and away from we visitors. Krause lit a cigarette and offered one to the man in uniform. The soldier ignored the gesture. Krause led me back the way we had come, and I relit my pipe. I hadn't noticed it going out while we were inspecting the border fence.

'Where did he come from?' I asked Krause.

'They patrol the true border from time to time. Probably we were spotted from one of the watchtowers and they signalled the soldier to take a look at us.' As we got back into the car, Krause told me that we would now go and see the fence in the town of Helmstedt.

I was somewhat puzzled for, as I tried to explain to my host, surely one sighting covers everything. This was different, Krause explained, for now we would see a crossing point, one of the few along the whole fence which went from the very north to the very south-east of the whole country.

As we drove into town, a watchtower came into view, intermittently blocked by various buildings as we drew closer.

'I want to stop here,' Krause said. 'We will walk the last little way. I don't want the guards to see my car.'

I was puzzled and asked why not.

'Because I drive into the East from time to time to see friends there and I don't want the GDR police to track my car numberplate and link my showing visitors this watchtower with my journeys to friends, who might then get implicated in something nasty.'

I understood immediately but was horrified to learn that such calculations were necessary. All very cloak and dagger. I felt rather sick. We walked on to the next street intersection, looked left and there, only about a hundred and fifty metres away, was a watchtower built adjacent to the road across which were some quite complex gates. With suitable papers, West Germans could walk or drive across into the East through those gates under the ever-watchful eyes of several (how many? I wondered) East German soldiers or policemen and women. Krause passed me a small pair of binoculars.

'Look up at the top of the tower,' he told me.

I slowly scanned the tower from bottom to top. As my view began to take in the platform at the top of the tower, what should I see but... someone with a pair of binoculars pointed at me.

'They have parabolic microphones, too,' Krause told me.

I waved at the soldier inspecting me and said, no doubt rather stupidly, 'Pity you have nothing better to do!' I returned the binoculars to Krause. After some minutes, he told me that we should go, and we did. I learned that my host crossed the border every couple of months or so. He had never had any difficulty but was always nervous doing it.

Krause drove me back to Wolfenbüttel. Neither of us spoke until my hotel came into view. This time there had been no tourist commentary whatsoever. Looking back, I think that our silence was as much due to my wish to be polite to an attentive host every bit as much as my finding difficulty in expressing what I thought after so moving an afternoon.

After we arrived at my hotel, Krause said that some post-docs from his laboratory would take me to dinner and entertain me for the evening. Then he bade me goodbye and bon voyage. I thanked him profusely for taking the trouble to show me the border. I assured him that it was an afternoon I would never forget.

It wasn't too long before I was met as promised. There were three of Krause's people to take me out. I cannot remember their names but do have a vague recollection of having met them that morning. They were a cheerful group and led me off to a nearby restaurant, well within walking distance of my hotel, where they had a table booked. Apart from some beers and a piece of succulent roast pork, I am unable to recall exactly what we all ate that evening. That is unusual for me for my love of my stomach usually guarantees detailed memories of these occasions. I was still preoccupied with the events of that afternoon.

I do have some detailed recall of what happened after we left the restaurant, bundled into a car and took off for someone's apartment. There were several more people already there, all men. Many beers were offered, and my hosts were totally relaxed and obviously happy to be hosting me for the evening. I grew somewhat more relaxed in their company. There was a lot of laughter and more animated conversation.

I thought that the humour was somewhat heavy-handed at times and was reminded of seeing an egg-and-spoon race conducted by families in some German town or other. The contrast with how it would happen in England was dazzling. The Germans took the whole thing very seriously and little Fritz was pushed forward and shouted at (not with) all the way. In England, such races were conducted instinctively with lots of laughter and gaiety with no real investment in the result. At another point in those German games, it was the turn of the wives and girlfriends to perform some running and jumping race but here, pairs of swarthy German lads and husbands took the ladies by their hands and arms and pulled them along in such a manner that I thought they might dislocate the girls' — admittedly beefy — arms from their sockets. I know we have that ridiculous game in England of wife-carrying, but at least the lasses are carried in one piece.

Then again, consider the English village cricket match. Teams dress up properly in their whites, and the field is surrounded on one side by spectators from the local village and from that of the opposing team, seated on deckchairs and sipping lemonade or the odd half-pint of mild or bitter. A fast bowl at the vicar is dealt with in a miraculous, if fluky, way and ends up over the boundary evincing some desultory applause. The vicar is bowled out by the following ball. As he strides back to the clubhouse, there is a broken ripple of applause from the thirty-strong crowd. 'Well played, Vicar!' is the call. Now that is how cricket should be played, I believe! None of this damn professionalism. It's a *game*, for God's sake. What's winning got to do with it? I am very well aware that many would disagree with my view, but I am entitled to it, nevertheless.

Back in Wolfenbüttel there came a point when I felt that I should offer a token of comradeship.

'My grandmother was German, you know,' I offered, and continued, 'She came from Bavaria to England when she was a young woman.'

'Oh, Bavaria isn't really Germany,' one of my young hosts protested, or Chermany as I heard. 'Vee in Saxony and Vestphalia are kvite different. You Enklish and we northern Chermans have the same sense of chooma!' he continued with some force.

I couldn't help it, but I had this memory pop up — but of course, it couldn't really have been a memory because it happened before I was born — about how, in 1936, I think it was, a delegation of Germans — Nazis, of course — visited some powerful Englishmen in the hope of forming a sort of alliance, emphasising common goals and outlook. They insisted along the way, that "We have the same values" and "You Enklish and we Chermans have a similar sense of chooma". Not bloody likely!

Next morning, after breakfast, I took a cab to Braunschweig rail station and began the first part of my return journey home by that short rail journey to Hanover, then by air to Amsterdam where I changed to a small aircraft which flew me direct to Cambridge. I was very pleased to get back home, but remained oddly quiet, for me at least, for several days. I just felt strangely ill at ease.

Part II

5

It was late summer/early autumn of 1989 before I took off on another lecture tour in Europe. There were the same aims as before except that this time I was considerably more ambitious. I planned to visit a former student, now professor, in Zaragoza in Spain; the nuclear research reactor in Grenoble; a chemist in Geneva who was famous within my field, a former colleague and co-author, also professor, in Basel in Switzerland; Rudolf Krause in Braunschweig again; and two laboratories in The Netherlands.

The first leg was to fly from Stansted to Madrid and then take the train to Zaragoza. I had never been to Spain before and had only a vague idea where its capital, Madrid, was situated. Larry Falvello, my host in Zaragoza, had given me directions about the short journey through Madrid, from airport to train station, a journey I took around four o'clock on a sunny Friday afternoon. I saw some of down-town Madrid but far too little to recall anything significant. I should have broken my journey in Madrid, if only for a day, just to get a look at the place, but I felt that I was going to be away from home long enough as it was.

Madrid is situated pretty close to the geographical centre of Spain. Zaragoza lies to the north-east, about sixty percent of the way to Barcelona on the Mediterranean coast. Zaragoza is the capital of Spain's north-eastern province of Aragon. By population, it is Spain's nineth largest city with a population of about three-quarters of a million people. It straddles the river Ebro whose waters derive from the Pyrenees, some hundred kilometres away to the north.

My journey by express train from Madrid to Zaragoza took about three hours, the light having gone by the time I reached my destination but not before I had looked out on some stunning old castle ruins atop rocky outcrops along the way. Many of these I saw in the low, golden and red lights of the setting sun so that they almost appeared as stage sets erected just for the benefit of the travellers, hurtling past.

The train arrived on time and I was met by Larry as arranged. He took me to the hotel in Zaragoza where I would stay for four nights, checked me in and left me to my own devices, but not before I learned about a small restaurant inside the hotel where I could get something to eat that evening. I had chosen to arrive on Friday so that I would have the weekend to explore the city before attending to my professional duties on Monday. Larry gave me a few pointers for my time on Saturday but asked me to leave Sunday noon onwards free so that he and his wife, Mila, could take me to lunch. My room was small but clean and well-appointed and I was happy. I had been worried about getting a meal at eight-thirty or even later but Larry gave me my first lesson in the way Spaniards live.

'Tapas from seven-thirty. Dinner might not begin till eleven in many places. You'll be fine in the hotel whenever you want to eat. They are used to foreigners.'

I had arrived with absolutely no idea of Spain's eating habits. Once again, outside of my speciality, I simply oozed a happy ignorance. My life has changed with experience, but experience, rather than reading, has been my teacher. Indeed, it was well after eight-thirty p.m. before I ambled into the hotel restaurant. It wasn't a posh affair, by any means, rather somewhat reminiscent of an American diner, for along one long wall, were set four-seater tables and benches at right angles to the wall. They were, on the other hand, set with tablecloths and the benches were cushioned. On the opposite side of the room, was a long bar with all the usual drinks behind it. It took me some time to become aware, however, of plates and bowls of food at a slightly lower level immediately behind the bar. I guessed that there were some twenty or so of these — all different. These, as we all now know of course, were the *tapas* for which Spanish cuisine is renowned; Spanish *hors d'oeuvres* which the locals consume with drinks during the early part of the evening, often with the intention of turning their attention to a full meal later; meaning ten-thirty or eleven p.m.

I could have joined in with the *tapas* and have been completely satisfied before turning in, but I had no idea what most of the dishes were or how much they would cost, and as usual, I had to watch the pennies. Moreover, I didn't speak a word of Spanish and everyone perched on the high stools in front of the bar — men with men, women with women,

women with men — was jabbering away, fifty to the dozen. I thought it simpler to sit alone at a table on the other side of the room. I was happy enough to do that. I ordered a beer and a steak and settled down to examine my companions as discreetly as I could.

It was only then that I spotted the most obvious thing in the room. Spaniards — in 1989 at least — were avid smokers. Nearly everyone at the bar was smoking a cigarette, even while eating, but as they finished their cigs, they squeezed the butts out and discarded them on the floor around them. It is absolutely no exaggeration to say that cigarette ends formed a carpet of half a metre wide and ten centimetres deep beneath their bar stools. It must immediately be said, however, that neither the room in general nor the patrons themselves were to be described as dirty or dishevelled. Every other thing about that restaurant was perfectly respectable, clean and wholesome. There was just this metres-long, deep pile of tab ends under the stools. You don't find that in guidebooks! I enjoyed my steak, lit my pipe, had another beer, and eventually went to bed and a satisfied sleep.

My Saturday had been planned to be my tourist day. After breakfast and armed with a small local map from the hotel concierge, I walked purposefully out of my resting place. I had learned from Larry before leaving Cambridge that a local cathedral had some frescoes painted by Goya on its ceiling. I had admired Goya for years, and despite my atheistic take on life, enjoyed church architecture, so my first port of call that morning was the Catedral-Basílica de Nuestra Señora del Pilar — Cathedral-Basilica of Our

Lady of the Pillar — which is probably the most obvious building in that city. It is very grand with a particularly impressive front facade and is reputed to be the first church in history to have been dedicated to the Virgin Mary.

It was another sunny morning, so it took a few moments for my eyes to acclimatise to the relative darkness within. There were several people inside but initially, my total attention was up towards the ceiling. At first, I was puzzled, for the decorations I saw were most certainly not impressive, not by Goya, nor were they in particularly good condition; they were quite dirty, I thought, undoubtedly from an accumulation of candle smoke, a well-known problem in churches around the world. However, there was much vaulting between the structural ribs in the arched roof and not all areas sported paintings by the master.

As I walked along, there came an abrupt change. Here were the Goyas, clean and well lit. Not too many of them but all quite magnificent. My neck began to hurt, so I found myself a chair and leaned back. I noticed that the figures were less elongated than I had become accustomed to from Goya paintings which I had seen in various galleries around the world. I spent a long time in that position so that my neck really ached by the time I had had my fill. If I had seen nothing else that morning, I would have been more than satisfied. But it was time to give my neck muscles a rest and look around the Basilica itself.

It was, indeed, very grand, but it was only then that I became aware of the significant volume of sound, of voices, all around me. Certainly, there were many obvious visitors in the place, wandering hither and thither, but by and large, they weren't responsible for the noise. No, that came from a service taking place nearby; no that wasn't right either, for the confusion of voices and their differing volumes revealed that there were several services, religious intonations or just plain mumblings of one kind or another going on from all parts of this very large basilica. I became aware that the whole cathedral nave was separated by iron lattice work and such, into distinct bays as it were, each being devoted to a different saint as evidenced by differing statuary and iconography and each being attended by small congregations of people sitting in chairs associated with each bay. In each area, was a table loaded with candles for sale — at what seemed exorbitant prices to me — for the faithful to offer up to their favourite saint. Behind or sometimes to the side of each such section were a couple of confessional boxes. On at least two occasions, I became aware of mumblings from these private places, all adding to the general background of noise in the basilica. As I wandered clockwise round the basilica, I saw similar gatherings in most of these discrete bays. The layout was rather like that of a marketplace — fish stall here, meat next, then vegetable produce... Roll up, roll up, ladies and gentlemen, buy a candle or two for your favourite saint here! Buy, buy.

La pièce de résistance, however, came at the end of my near-circular tour, for there I found a church within a church, as it were. Much more spacious than the bays I had been looking at, this last environment had a double area of seating with an aisle between them; an alter with a cross, large candles and all the things one might otherwise expect upon it; and a priest holding forth to a not inconsiderable congregation of worshipers. Indeed, a mass was being held and acts of communion were taking place in front of the alter. As one priest finished his part, he was replaced by another, then another. Other clerics in full regalia went among the congregation, loudly rattling large money boxes, and the believers were making their contributions. Once more, at the back of this church-within-a-church, was placed a table, wider than before, laden with candles larger than before, at prices higher than before. The rattling of the collection boxes seemed to fill the air like a barrel organ. Buy, buy!

I had attended a Church of England school before my eleventh year — for no better reason, by the way, than that it was the closest to my home and necessitated my crossing no main roads each day as I walked to school — and had been taught about Christ throwing market traders out of the church, tipping their tables up and tossing their wares onto the ground in his anger. But this was different, wasn't it? Was it? I had my opinion. I left the Grand Basilica in some disgust.

At that time, most Spaniards were baptised as Catholics and a large percentage practised their religion faithfully throughout their lives. Mind you, only a few years before my visit to Zaragoza, church and state had been officially separated, and in the years since, Church power and influence have waned markedly. In any case, I was only too aware that my impressions of Catholicism that day were obviously affected by place. If not in the Great Basilica, where else would you expect to see such a following? Place will always affect one's conclusions.

Time was getting on and I felt in need of a spot of lunch and went in search of a cheap *restaurante*. I was by no means sure that anything resembling lunch would be served at one p.m. after my experiences of the previous evening but there was no problem, probably because these places were well used to tourists.

After a pleasant break, I simply wandered at random as was my habit. Had I been a proper tourist and done my homework, I would have discovered the El Tubo district of old Zaragoza, filled with eateries of various kinds but specialising in *tapas* in the evenings. I might have visited the most beautiful Aljaferia Palace. But I didn't. I did find a fabulous shoe shop, the description of which made my wife's eyes water when I told her on my return home. I also found an interesting cheese and wine shop in which the ground floor was given over to cheeses and the basement, or cellar, to wines. I made a short meander through this emporium and was suitably impressed. After a while, I felt weary, found a park and sat down on a bench for a while. All in all, a simple exploration which led me back to my hotel by mid-afternoon but not before I had surveyed the immediate neighbourhood in search of a restaurant for the evening.

Back in my hotel, after a quick shower upstairs, I found my way into the hotel lobby where I settled into a deep, soft armchair and picked up a local newspaper. I was curious as whether I could glean anything at all using my non-existent Spanish. To my considerable surprise, I found myself able to get the drift, at least, of many of the headlines. That was something I had been totally unable to do with some Italian newspapers I had sampled in Florence, and it came as a surprise. I had expected things to be the other way round; that Spanish would be completely strange to me. Once more, I thought, it's so easy to form a prejudice from nothing at all. I couldn't really make much headway with the actual articles in the newspaper, but I did feel a frisson of pleasure in getting as far as I did.

A young lady from the main desk came up to me to ask if I would like a drink. Goodness knows why I made the choice I did late-afternoon that day, but I asked for a Cointreau. The lady went away but returned in short order to enquire whether I would like that with a cordial. God no! I thought and said, 'No thanks, just straight, as it is, nothing added at all, thanks.'

It was plain that she had absolutely no idea about Cointreau at all when she reappeared with a brandy balloon, *half-full* of the delicious liqueur. I sipped and found that it was the real thing and there I was with probably a six-fold measure of the stuff in my glass. I wondered just what I was going to be charged for my drink but put that thought aside for the moment. I enjoyed a most pleasant and relaxed afternoon. Before returning to my room before dinner, I paid for my Cointreau and was amazed to be charged merely the equivalent of what I would have paid back home for the customary single measure, traditionally served in a small liqueur glass. Then I set forth for my evening meal in that place I had discovered just round the corner. I found a paella

— or small version of one — on offer and decided on that. And a nice rioja. By nine o'clock, I returned to my hotel, a happy man indeed.

Larry and Mila met me in the lobby just after eleven thirty a.m. the next day — Sunday — as arranged. Larry Falvello had joined me from a background as a crystallographer — an area in which I had specialised for my own doctorate several years earlier — to study for his PhD. Larry is an American from Pennsylvania with an Italian family background. He had been an excellent student, not only clever, but had an extremely likeable character and he got on well with my other students as well as with me. The time came, after being awarded his doctorate, that Larry — now a post-doctoral fellow and still working with me — expressed the wish to return to the States sometime soon, and he asked me if I could help him find a suitable billet.

I wrote to a very senior American chemist, Al Cotton at Texas A&M in America whom I had known for many years and asked if he might have a slot for a man with Larry's background. It was a bit of a long shot, but Al had many people in his group and was, I thought, likely to have a bit of spare cash — grant money — lying around. Actually, that was something of an optimistic try, but you never know. Well, to cut a long story very short indeed, my mark came up trumps, and after some months, Larry joined the great man in Texas as his crystallographer. For a couple of years, Larry was just a valued, competent post-doctoral fellow in Al's group, but gradually he began to run the great man's whole crystallographic enterprise. It was there that Larry met an attractive visiting post-doc from Spain, and in due course... they married. Mila suggested that Larry apply for a professorship at the University of Zaragoza, one of the oldest and most highly regarded of Spain's academic, research institutions. Larry was offered and accepted the job, and at the time of my visit, had been in place for just a few months. That Sunday was the first time that I had met Mila. I knew immediately that we would get on and I hoped that my approval of Larry's choice, not that it was at all needed, was apparent.

It turned out that the restaurant Larry had in mind was but a ten-minute, sunny walk away from my hotel. It was a bright and airy place, quite modern and pretty large. At twelve noon there were already several diners around. Having only recently learned something of Spanish eating habits, I hadn't expected to see that but Sunday lunch, as I was about to discover, is something special. Roughly centrally placed in that room was what looked like a very large bread oven, obviously constructed of brick and covered with rough render. No doubt the temperature inside was high — it must have been, judging by the luscious smells coming from the small opening at the front — and although the brick and render would be expected to insulate the whole thing, I felt a wave of warmth as we passed by to reach our table. Larry told me that there would be lamb roasting inside that oven. The smells only confirmed this.

We had barely settled when Larry caught the attention of a waiter and ordered a bottle of champagne. Larry was obviously in a mood to celebrate — his new job, his wife, his visitor. I was proud to be there. A mood of quiet pleasure grew at our table, a mood that was to become quite soporific by the end of the afternoon. I more or less left the choosing to Larry. We began with some *gambas*, which I already knew meant prawns. A lovely thing to accompany the champagne, I thought. Larry asked me if I'd like to try the garlic soup. I was a little hesitant but thought, why not? Well, I soon found out the answer to that. The soup was intensely rich in garlic, but since we were having lamb afterwards, I didn't mind that too much. What I didn't like was the greasiness, maybe oiliness, of the soup.

It reminded me forcefully of the chicken soup an aunt of mine regularly served up to me whenever I visited her home — with or without my parents. My dad didn't really get on too well with this particular lady and would try to avoid being a lunch or dinner guest at her place. The trouble was that he was often dragooned into doing the odd job around the place for this maidenly sister-in-law and she insisted on "rewarding" him for his efforts. And she invariably served up a bowl of chicken soup. The trouble was that she never removed the over-plentiful grease which had come from the long-boiled bird, with the result that a layer of fat, a millimetre or more thick, covered the whole of the soup. That had two consequences, every spoonful tasted strongly of the fatty grease, and the surface layer of oil kept in the heat of the soup. I always burned my tongue when supping that offering. Well, the Spanish garlic soup was rather like that. I manfully tried to do it justice (maybe more than justice!) but gave in eventually.

Larry sympathised and we moved on to the main course and a bottle of *rioja*. All three of us were taking the lamb. A waiter brought a beautiful-looking cut of lamb to our table. It smelled divine, it had a crispy skin, and it was oozing blood and all things gorgeous. I expected the waiter to put the joint on the table ready for carving or, maybe, to take it away for carving. To my astonishment, however, he attacked the lamb on the platter, resting on the trolley upon which it had appeared, and shredded the whole thing with a pair of forks, much as the Chinese will shred a duck for that lovely pancake dish, we call Peking duck. I considered this manoeuvre to be a sacrilege. I like to cut up my own piece of lamb for myself. Oh well, when in Rome… or Spain, as was the case here. The meat tasted superb, however, so I had to put down the strange procedure to "foreign ways". Only much later did I discover the concept of "pulled" pork, or lamb in this case.

It was a wonderful meal, and somewhere along the line, I could swear that a second bottle of rioja appeared. We had some sweet afterwards but I simply cannot remember what it was. Coffee followed that, together with a liqueur under Larry's insistence, and Larry brought forth a couple of quite superb cigars. Sometime after all this was consumed — talking, reminiscing and laughing all the while — we made our move. As we walked out of the restaurant, I glanced at my watch. It was nearly six o'clock! We had spent close to six hours gorging ourselves and every moment had been like soaking in a hot bath. What a wonderful afternoon! I did little more that day, taking myself off to bed quite early.

Larry picked me up after breakfast the following morning to take me off to his department where I was scheduled to give my research lecture. I was pleased to see a good turn-out, and wondered if Larry had put out the hard word. Larry introduced me to the audience. He spoke for about four minutes in Spanish. As usual on these lecture tours, I wondered at the linguistic skills of my hosts. It seemed that they were all happy to speak English to me, and of course — but I realise that there was no "of course" about it — I always delivered my lecture in English. Certainly, English is the predominant language of science throughout the world and I am only too grateful for being English because of that, if for no other reason. But here was my former student, an American from Texas, only recently in his new job as professor in Zaragoza, speaking what certainly sounded to me like "joined-up" Spanish in his introduction. Apart from the occasional mention of my name, or my subject, or by virtue of the odd gesture, I had absolutely no idea what was being said. Larry finished his little speech — for that is what it was, after all — by relaxing into his native tongue to formally introduce me and ask me to give my lecture.

I began by thanking my audience for tolerating my lack of Spanish and by promising them not to talk too fast. This was a usual opening when I toured in Europe. Afterwards, I felt that I had been understood well enough and that there had been a modicum of interest. I never expected more than that. Sometimes, I would meet up with someone whose work was particularly close to my own and then conversations would become quite animated. I shared a simple lunch with Larry and some of his group and spent some time talking with Larry's research students about ligand-field theory and Cambridge. I left Zaragoza immediately after an early breakfast next day, ready to meet my next hosts.

6

I caught the Madrid to Barcelona train, the one which had deposited me in Zaragoza on Friday, arriving in Barcelona about an hour later. I would so like to have made a stop in that wonderful city but just couldn't afford the time. I got as far as walking out of the station in Barcelona onto a huge concourse in the warm sun only to turn back in search of my connection to Grenoble which left shortly afterwards.

As we sped through Figueres, I remembered that it was the birthplace of the surrealist, Salvador Dali, whose paintings had first come to my attention in my student days in London. One of the most breath-taking things I had ever seen at that point in my, admittedly inexperienced, life was Dali's *Metamorphosis of Narcissus*. Apart from the humour in the image, what had stuck in my memory more than anything else was the iridescence of that painting in the Tate gallery. I often wondered whether that was simply down to clever spotlighting in the gallery, but I think it is more than that. I couldn't take my eyes off that picture. It was soon after that, when I found a biography of the great man by Fleur Cowles called *The Case of Salvador Dali*. Even as I read through this quite lengthy book — long for me at that stage in my woefully ill-read life — I became aware that I wasn't reading a deep account. I was also aware that Dali was a superb self-publicist, something which, I'm afraid, has always stuck in my throat. I make this remark as a simple description of how I feel, I am not at all sure that I could defend the position in argument. On the other hand, Dali's public behaviour was at one with his painting and surrealist ideals, if that's an appropriate word for them. All these thoughts flooded through my mind in a hazy sort of way as the train sped through Figueres but there was one more, utterly trivial memory which was as sharp as a tack.

I have always been a slow reader. I can read quickly if it becomes necessary, but I enjoy taking my time, soaking in the words. I often used to pop into coffee bars in South Kensington, as did many of my fellow students from Imperial College in those days. Coffee bars were the thing then. I doubt if the name means much today. I would stroll down to South Ken in the evening, and on some occasions, would be tempted into ordering a small meal as well as coffee, even though I had already eaten in the college canteen. I was carrying my copy of the Dali book and began to read it while waiting for my meal. I remember ordering a dish called *julskinka*. I did not know what *julskinka* really was except that it was Swedish. This version of *julskinka* turned out to be a reasonably thick slice of warm ham spread with marmalade. I enjoyed it well enough and wonder now if I remember that dish simply because of repeating the strange name over and over till I got it into my head. Sounds likely.

Anyway, the point of this pedestrian little tale comes when it was time to pay the bill, for I reached into my pocket only to discover that I had forgotten to pick up my wallet before I'd left my digs. Actually, that's quite odd really because I rarely forget anything, and I have discussed this event with friends on more than one occasion because of that. It seems that my forgetfulness is rare, yet I remember the occasions when it happens with acute... shame almost. In recent years, as an old man, my memory is still sharp, but the blanks occur more often, and when they do, seem to be total. Well, there I was without the ability to pay for my supper. I explained my circumstances to the coffee-bar owner and told him that I lived in Drayton Gardens, that I would run back, pick up my wallet, and return in about half-an-hour. I thought to convince the bar-owner of my honesty by offering — no insisting, actually — on leaving my precious Fleur Cowles book as surety on the counter. I doubt that the bar-owner was in the least impressed. But I insisted with so much sincerity, and anyway, the man could do little else but accept the token, and I dashed off. I ran all the way home, picked up my wallet (checking that there was money inside) and ran all the way back. It took me about thirty-five minutes before I reclaimed my precious volume, and very slowly now, walked from the bar.

All that, as my train sped through the last town of any size on the Spanish side of the Spanish/French border. Later on, as we reached Avignon, yet another memory came back. Train journeys do that to you, don't you think? This one was of an occasion when I was travelling with my wife, Gwyneth, from Barcelona to Paris. We had arranged to break our journey for a couple of days to stay with some dear friends who lived in Verneuil-en-Bourbonnais, a village in the

Auvergne. It has a population of rather less than three hundred people. Gwyn and I had instructions to change trains after Avignon off the main drag and to alight — by prior arrangement with the guard — at a place whose name I cannot remember or find on the map; yet another blank! That's a pity, as we'll see from what follows.

We had taken an earlier train than originally arranged, arriving at our mystery station — "the French equivalent of Crewe", our hosts had told us — with a couple of hours to spare. I took a few steps outside the station to see what was around but there wasn't much as far as I could see. I had hoped to find a nice bistro for lunch, for it was that time of day. As I turned back towards the station, I realised that a building behind the station, or rather a part of it attached in T formation, sported the sign "restaurant". I poked my head in, liked what I saw and collected Gwyn from where she was guarding our luggage.

The place turned out to be far grander inside than we had any right to expect. It had tall windows lighting a double-storey space; quite cavernous, indeed. There were many tables arranged in a somewhat formal pattern, each being neatly covered with a good damask tablecloth and all laid, as far as I could see, with cutlery and glasses, ready to go. We found ourselves a convenient spot and sat down. I examined the menu which was quite extensive. I had the brainwave to suggest the *plat du jour*, a beef braise, arguing that if that's what this place said was today's special it would be churlish not to take it up. We also ordered a bottle of red to go with the braised beef to come.

Gwyn looked around the place and pointed out to me, as I had my back to them, library-style bookcases completely filled with interesting-looking volumes; in French, no doubt, but Gwyn's love of books was aroused by the sight. There was a low buzz of sound in the place which made for a happy atmosphere, rather than strong echoes which might have been expected, perhaps, with so high a ceiling. There was no sign of special soundproofing. The place just worked as it should.

Our meal arrived in due course as a sizeable roll of beef which looked no better than a cheap brisket or some such. I cut into the roll, expecting some heavy resistance but was pleasantly surprised to find that it cut like butter. It tasted delicious and the sauce which came with it only served to make a very good dish, sublime. We were very happy bunnies indeed. It seemed churlish not to follow this unexpected wonder by dessert, so I chose a tart and Gwyn, some chevre. We were feeling very lucky and content as we made our way to pay the modest bill and to discover that the restaurant was not only attached to the railway station but was, in fact, also accessed through the simple platform buffet we had seen on our arrival but rejected in favour of something outside. What a find. When John and Danielle, our hosts, drove up to collect us and take us to their home, we blabbered incessantly about our good fortune.

John Lyons was a colleague of mine; indeed, he was the master of my college, Trinity Hall. We had all been friends for some time and Gwyn and I had heard wonderful reports about what John and Danielle had done with their "country retreat". They had displayed a keen sense of style in their home in Cambridge as well as in the Master's Lodge so we were most curious.

The village of Verneuil-en-Bourbonnais was exquisite. Narrow lanes between substantial stone houses, a generous green in the middle, and everything was so neat and well-cared-for. We were surprised to find that John and Danielle's house was semi-detached. We had expected a detached place at the very least. Obviously, this holiday home — which was to become their only home in a few years, however — was just a modest affair. Just shows how wrong you can be. Inside, this four- maybe five-storey house was anything but modest. The rooms were very large, both in height and area, and the oak ceiling beams were some of the most substantial that Gwyn and I had ever seen. John told us that the wall separating them from their neighbours was some two or more metres thick. They heard absolutely nothing from next door. More than that, towards the front of the house where the separating wall was at its thickest, John had his builder cut into it and carve out an alcove large enough to put a small table and a couple of chairs, and still all on their side of the formal divide.

John and Danielle had been working on this property for some years now. It was a listed building and they had found a builder who was an expert in renovating such old places while in keeping within the endless rules set up by the French authorities. He was a man of great taste and considerable imagination. Most of the room walls were covered in hessian — mounted on a wooden frame backing — which had been stiffened and painted — dark grey in our bedroom; elsewhere dark blue or dark green — but in such a way that the hessian was stretched, and its weave not filled with congealed paint. It was immaculately done, and their builder/designer had won some award or other for his work and ideas. This was a show-house in the best sense of that phrase.

John and Danielle were very proud of their home and justly so. They gave us a tour of the place, knowing how interested we were in house design. Their own bedroom was very large and decorated in a manner fit for a king (and his queen). However, just as Gwyn and I cannot share a kitchen, John and Danielle could not share a bathroom. So they had one each, Danielle's being en suite to their bedroom, and John's a little way off, up a circular stone staircase leading from it. Further up that stairway, was situated a large, sunny gym. This too, had segregated areas containing the favoured equipment of these two, strong-willed protagonists. Their bedroom had a large, stone balcony with views over their garden and the village around. And so it went. Four bedrooms in all, each almost more beautiful than the last; most en suite. And the main rooms downstairs, lounge, dining and kitchen were all, and more than, you could hope for. It was a magnificent house, and we were made completely welcome. The highlight of the property, perhaps, was the garden. There was a stone balcony outside the lounge and directly under a similar structure outside our hosts' bedroom, overlooking it. It was a courtyard garden.

The house was roughly in the middle of the village and had little land. Instead, there was a courtyard bounded by the house itself; thick, high walls between them and their neighbours; and a small stable block behind, which John and Danielle were using for storage at that time. Again, all walls were built of gorgeous thick stone. The stable block was tiled with old terracotta pantiles. Apparently when they had bought the place, the yard was full of rubble and muck. They had worked their socks off to bring it to the stage it now was, and in doing so, revealed a lovely stone floor throughout the courtyard. The final and crowning glory, however, was the rose planting by Danielle, who had shown similar subtle taste in the college gardens back in Cambridge. All round the courtyard, was a narrow strip of soil. Danielle had chosen some of France's most delicious climbing roses to fill that strip of garden. She had been so restrained in her palette — whites, creams and soft pinks. One rose, however, though quite lovely in itself, did stand out as a rogue. It was deep pink, and it stuck out like a sore thumb.

'It will have to go!' Danielle insisted, 'As soon as the season is finished, it's coming out.'

She was quite right. Mind you, nobody is perfect I mused, and was just a teeny bit pleased to find a chink in our friends' otherwise, all too solid armour.

Later, we sat in the late afternoon sun, sipping a glass of wine and chatting about old friends. Our meal that night was that great French classic, *coq au vin*. Danielle, who had lived with John in England for many years, even before he became master of Trinity Hall, was well aware of the lackadaisical manner in which many English cooks prepare this dish. Danielle, however, was having none of that, insisting that the *coq* had indeed, to be an old cock rather than a common-or-garden young chook, and she had sought one out from a nearby farmer she knew. She did us proud that evening.

Next day, John and Danielle took Gwyn and me out for a walk through their village which was every bit as picturesque as a first glance had promised. We bumped into a local man, a near-neighbour, and he and John rattled off in French after introductions. I should mention, by the way, that Danielle was French, and John was English, and a (famous) linguist by profession. Danielle was very happy for them to retire in England where they had lived all of their married lives, but John was hell-bent on retiring in Danielle's home country, and as we shall see, Danielle favoured Verneuil-en-Bourbonnais.

Our party moved on and we wandered onto the village green, in the middle of which was a memorial to those lost in the two world wars. Gwyn and I spent a few moments looking at the names carved into the stone plinth which was somewhat more than a metre high. There were many names, so very many names. Danielle noticed our sombre mood and asked if we had lost relatives in the wars. We had not, but our sympathy for those who had, was genuine enough. I have always been immensely moved by thoughts of soldiers *and* civilians lost in war.

It was later, however, while taking us for a drive in the beautiful countryside, that Danielle again brought up the memorial. She was sitting with Gwyn on the rear seats while John and I were nattering up front, but I heard most of what Danielle had to say. She was talking about her grandmother who, it seems, had been an important figure in the Resistance in the Vichy district which included the village in which they now lived. Indeed, their village had been the local, but secret, centre of the Resistance — a quiet village being safely out of the way of the important Vichy town centre — and her grandmother, whose memory Danielle revered greatly, had either set up that branch or had been very senior in its leadership. Apparently, she had been enormously brave, saved many French lives and cost many German ones. The Resistance, after all, was an army of soldiers in kind, and war is war. Less than one hour after the cease-fire had been announced following the German surrender in May 1945, a German soldier shot — that is, murdered — Danielle's grandmother. Presumably the secret of her name or whereabouts, or both, were revealed too readily after the cease-fire. A street in Vichy is named in her honour.

7

Memories can be triggered by place, by people, or by anything at all really, I mused, as my train sped through Avignon that afternoon. After thinking about John and Danielle, my thoughts drifted to his predecessor as master of Trinity Hall. Morris Sugden retired early from academe as a reader in physical chemistry many years before I came to hear about, and ultimately, know him. He had a somewhat swarthy countenance, was invariably a little untidy, but the ever-present twinkle in his eye won him friends from all walks of life. Some people are like that, aren't they? I feel so jealous of their good fortune. Very, very sadly for everybody, Morris died in his early sixties from pancreatic cancer. He'd been a rather heavy drinker and many of us had helped him continue to enjoy his wicked habit. Roy Calne, the Fellow and surgeon I mentioned earlier, had cut Morris open to find out what his problem was. One look at his pancreas was all he needed to know Morris's fate.

'But,' he told me one day, months after Morris's death, 'while I was in there, I thought I should take a quick peek at his liver — drinker that he was. I nipped off just a small piece and sent it to the lab. His liver was in perfect shape!' Moral, things that might do you harm, might just not.

By the way, Gwyn and I ended up living in the same village, in the same lane even, in which Morris and Marion, his most talented wife — and by then, widow — had chosen a cottage for their retirement.

However, my memory during that train journey past Avignon concerned something from earlier days. After the Master's Lodge had been redecorated and such when Morris took over, he made an unusual use of a large room on the ground floor. Unusual, that is, for the master of a Cambridge College. He installed a half-size snooker table. He then let it be known that all members of the college were invited to make use of it at any time; and by all, he meant Fellows and college servants alike. That gesture was greatly appreciated "below stairs".

As I intimated earlier, Morris had had a successful career in academe. At the time of his retirement from that role, his reputation as a flame chemist (what goes on chemically in flames) was second to none throughout the world. He had followed his time in Cambridge by joining ICI as a research director so had been something of a bigwig in industry as well. When the position of master became vacant on the retirement of his predecessor, Morris was elected with spectacular enthusiasm. With his background as an industry director as well as a Cambridge academic, Trinity Hall won a strong man. Win-win, all round.

It was the way of things in those days, still to address the Boss by his proper title — Master. We had invariably done that for his predecessor, Alex Deer — a most friendly man, by the way — and we continued the habit for Morris. But only during the day and early part of the evening in the Fellows' common room. Now it was usual on Fellowship night, as I have mentioned briefly already, for post-prandial activity to continue for a long time. There was a seemingly endless supply of port, claret and sweet Barsac, for example, smoking was rife in those days, and there was snuff; what can you expect? Conversation — about the sublime as well as the cor-blimey — carried on for hours. However, several of us occasionally fancied a game of snooker after about nine o'clock and would slope off to that table in the Master's Lodge.

On that journey past Avignon, I was remembering one occasion when about eight of us decided to push some balls around in the dog hours of the evening and one of those eight was Morris Sugden himself. As soon as we reached the snooker room, glasses in hand, carafes in others' hands, we removed our gowns (always worn on Fellowship nights, of course) and settled quickly into two "sides". Of course, a game of snooker between two sides of four players each clearly defines a giggle match. At that stage in the evening, we should care! I ended up leading the opposition to Morris's team. I was smoking my pipe, as usual, and Morris, who had removed his jacket to reveal a handsome pair of braces, was smoking a half-corona cigar. Naturally, all formality was discarded, and Christian names were the order of the day (night?).

Morris was lining up for his shot, bent low over the baize, cigar manoeuvred to the side of his mouth, sliding his cue back and forth between the bridge of his left forefinger and thumb. But he was a little careless and his cue tip touched and slightly moved the cue ball.

'Foul,' I exclaimed from the side of the table, for it was. Morris didn't stand up, but maintaining his position, he paused for a moment and his head merely swivelled in my direction.

'Bugger off!' he said in a slow, firm but quiet voice, turned back and took his shot.

I laughed in great joy at this wanton and brazen act of bastardry.

'Is this a case of *droit du seigneur*?' I asked.

'Too right!' he replied.

Well, it was his snooker table, and he was master.

The last hour of my journey to Grenoble was especially spectacular, though not, perhaps, as breath-taking as that from Lyon to Grenoble which I had taken on earlier visits to this gateway to the French ski fields. Not that I am a skier — except in the sense I learned about many years later just before retirement when introduced to the acronym, to SKI means to Spend the Kids' Inheritance. No, the last few tens of kilometres to that lovely city lie through the mountains leading to the French Alps proper, and at one point, the railway line snaked along the sides of steep slopes leading down to exquisite, glass-like lakes. Grenoble itself is built around the confluence of the Isere and Drac rivers. On the left, just before pulling into Grenoble station from the east, the train passes a high cliff or rock. Otherwise, the land is flat for at least a kilometre around so that rock is a most obvious and memorable landmark. To use a greatly overused label; it is iconic of the approach to Grenoble station.

I planned to spend only a couple of days in Grenoble. Much as I liked the place, I couldn't really afford more time there on this occasion. John Davies, one of my postdoctoral Fellows, was running an experiment at the Institut Laue-Langevin. The ILL is situated in that flat area on the right of the train tracks in between the two rivers. The whole area is known as the Polygone Scientifique and houses several important laboratories as well as the most obvious feature from a tourist's point of view, the ILL nuclear reactor dome. It was in that building that my colleague was working. The institute is named after two physicists, Max von Laue from Germany and Paul Langevin from France.

The powerful reactor inside that building was built as a research facility to provide an intense source of neutrons which may be exploited in all manner of scientific experiments within physics, chemistry, biology and material sciences. From a scientific point of view, the importance of this facility lies in the high intensity of the neutron stream, or flux, that it produces. At that time, only a laboratory at Brookhaven in the States could rival this flux. Britain has a research reactor in Oxfordshire but an experiment there could take months while at the ILL, it might take only hours.

My experiment used polarised neutrons for which the effective flux is less by several orders of magnitude. My colleague and I were lucky to be allocated a three-week slot at the reactor and even that only allowed for a quarter of what needed to be done. I could tell you that the experiment has to do with hurling minute magnets at a magnetic material and watching how they are scattered, but I won't. Anyway, this isn't a scientific tale so that's all you get, folks.

The business of producing the neutron flux was all in the hands of local staff, nuclear engineers, physicists and their specialised assistants. Visiting experimenters are responsible for providing a sample (a large single crystal in my case) and for recording the direction of the scattered neutrons using computerised facilities provided by the institute. So much of the work, after an initial setting-up of the experiment, is computerised and automatic, and goes on twenty-four hours a day without any need of supervision. Consequently, when I visited my postdoc, there was plenty of time to talk about progress as well as to go into town for more talk, recreation and a meal.

The ILL, by the way, was funded jointly by France, Germany and the UK. Actually, it was supported only by France and Germany in its beginning. That was why its name honours scientists from those two countries only. Later, Britain joined in the enterprise — and funding — and this led to an interesting arrangement so far as formal control is concerned. The chairmanship of the institute rotates, or oscillates perhaps, between Britain and Germany but not France, the reason being that the centre had been built on French soil with all the practical advantages that brought — such as everyday staff to run the place being recruited from local sources, for example — so presenting a sort of standing gain to the host country. Anyway, that's the way it was. In truth, the ILL is an international facility although the three financing countries take the lion's share of the facilities.

It is quite amazing, by the way, that the reactor was built in that location in the first place. Reactors are dangerous things, and if anything serious were to go wrong, like a leakage of radiation from the reactor core, for example, imagine how dangerous that would be to the city lying only a kilometre away and to the hinterland with the River Isere taking contaminants for hundreds of kilometres. All proper precautions were taken, of course, and there never has been any even vaguely serious problem but...

The city of Grenoble is a beautiful place. It has some very old buildings and the place actually goes back two thousand years. There are some good restaurants around — always a plus for me, of course — and this was where I first encountered that simple, but so delightful, signature dish of this, the Dauphine region, namely, *pommes* — or *gratin* — *dauphinois*. I had first visited Grenoble in my post-doctoral years when money was pretty tight so that *gratin* stays firmly in my mind as a cheap way to eat first-rate grub. I was also fond of a pizzeria on the banks of the Isere close to where the Téléphérique cable car, affectionately known as *les bulles* (the bubbles) to the locals because of the line of small, almost spherical cabins which move up the cables to the summit of a local rock called the Bastille. I was once driven up to the top of the system and discovered that the view of Grenoble from there is quite stunning. I never took the cable car myself, however, from a long-standing fear of anything high or seemingly unsupported. Strange, though, that I have never had any fear of flying.

On this occasion, John Davies and I found time to relax for an afternoon after catching up with our professional project. We sat in a little café in the centre of the old town, watching tennis from Wimbledon on a television set which was suspended from the ceiling. Other patrons were only too relieved when the match finished. We ate a *croque monsieur* washed down with a beer or two. I consider it to be rather more subtle than a Welsh rarebit.

My next but one port of call was to be Basel in Switzerland. It was surely one of the most beautiful journeys I had ever taken — Chambery, Geneva at the south end of Lake Geneva, Lausanne at the north end, and on to Basel. First, however, was my stopover in Geneva, which is to be counted as the capital of the French-speaking part of Switzerland. Berne, of course, is the real capital.

I had been to Geneva many years earlier, long before I had begun all these lecture tours. I found Geneva to be just as I remembered it, quite magisterial with all those magnificent hotels around the lake and that iconic fountain in the lake itself. As I walked through the station towards the street exit, I spotted the person who had arranged to meet me there. We had never met before, but it was abundantly clear to me that I had found my man.

That man was Christian Klixbull Jørgensen. What a name! He was a Dane who had competed with my friend, and executioner, Carl Ballhausen for the chair of theoretical chemistry at the Ørsted Institute in Copenhagen. Ballhausen had won. Ballhausen despised Jørgensen, and Jørgensen despised, and maybe even hated Carl Ballhausen. All this scuttlebutt had been common currency in Copenhagen during several of my visits there. I greatly admired Ballhausen and felt sure that the Danes had made the right choice. However, it had nothing to do with me, but since Jørgensen's work was very close to mine — I was his junior by many years, and certainly, in reputation — I was very keen to meet this man. It had been agreed that I would deliver a lecture on my work and spend some time "at the feet of the master".

Well, there waiting for me at Geneva station was a wispy-grey-haired man of slight stature, a little stooped, wearing an overlength mac and carrying a string bag. I assure you that there are many academics who don't look like that but Jørgensen fitted at least one stereotype to perfection.

Jørgensen welcomed me very briefly and then immediately began talking about ligand-field theory, our mutual speciality. Apart from a "welcome", that was the extent of small talk on offer. He led me to a bus stop, gabbling all the time. We climbed on board in due course, and Jørgensen's babbling continued. Worse, he held forth in a loud voice and every other passenger in the bus kept looking and quite obviously wishing that the silly man would shut up. I glanced at one of them and gave a watery smile.

The bus took us close to the university where we alighted and took a short walk into the great man's laboratory to find a couple of his students chatting. There were brief introductions, and at last, a few enquiries about my journey and other pleasantries. Jørgensen disappeared after a while, I was offered a lab coffee, and eventually my hosts took me through to the lecture theatre where I was to deliver my talk.

This was likely to be a test, for everyone in the audience was a Jørgensen disciple and thoroughly clued up on the details of his model, a model which I had adapted, changed and then criticised in print, several times! I was listened to and when question time came, I was given a pretty thorough going over. But they were fair, and nobody was rude. Whether I convinced anyone there of the superiority of my approach is anyone's guess, but these things take time. Afterwards, a couple in the audience took me for lunch in the cafeteria and they continued to discuss my talk until it was time to take me to see Jørgensen once more.

I was left with his secretary in a smart, well-furnished and large, outer office. After a moment, she took me through into the great man's lair. His office was easily twice the size of the outer vestibule. However, it had absolutely none of the dignity of that room. There was no desk for a start. Right in the middle of the room were two plain, simple and uncomfortable-looking, wooden chairs with wooden seats. They were placed directly facing each other about a metre apart. There was empty space around these chairs for a couple of metres, I would guess. All round the room, except for the door through which we had entered and another similar door in an adjacent wall, which Jørgensen himself no doubt used if he wished to bypass his secretary, were simple tables with metal legs and presumably Formica tops. I presume they were made of Formica because of their utilitarian appearance, otherwise, I was unable to tell because every last square inch of those tabletops was piled high with reprints of scientific papers. Behind most of the tables, bookcases were jammed full of books and yet more reprints.

For readers who may be unfamiliar with such reprints let me explain. When a scientist or research group publishes an article describing their work and theories, that article, or paper, appears in some learned journal or other. The author, or authors, are also sent — often not free of charge, by the way — a number of copies of that paper. These are sent out, on request, to fellow researchers around the world. Most scientists, however, are happy just to read a paper in the journal itself, only requesting a copy if they are very closely concerned with the field and anticipate referring to it frequently. Even then, given that that photocopiers are *de rigueur* in all university departments, most researchers are happy enough to settle for such a copy. But some there are who simply must have a nice, printed version and they send their requests to author(s) at considerable postage cost and much effort on their secretary's part, as like as not. I say like as not, because it is usually only professors who have access to funding for such pursuits. Well, Jørgensen's tables were littered with the things. There must have been thousands of them, for the piles all around were often half a metre thick.

I was invited to sit in the chair opposite the great man's who then launched into a general reverie about whatever topic momentarily had his attention. I immediately saw that such was the butterfly nature of his mind, for he kept hopping from one unrelated subject to another. It was fun in a way, and it was clear that I was not expected to make much of a contribution. Jørgensen did, however and somewhat obliquely, make reference to my lecture by congratulating me on some work in magnetism which I had done many years earlier. That work had not been part of my lecture. The implication was clear, my host liked my earlier work but not what I was doing now. The criticism was made in a perfectly polite way, and after all, Jørgensen was entitled to his view. In any case, I had criticised his work in print so why shouldn't he have a go?

At several points in his wide-ranging monologue, Jørgensen would suddenly ask — to nobody in particular, mind — 'Oh! Where was that paper published?' He would promptly answer his own question with something like, 'Ah! Yes. *Journal of Polish Chemistry*, 1956, Volume 43, page 19. Bottom of the right-hand column, I think,' and would immediately jump up from his chair and walk directly to one of the tables around the walls, reach under a pile on the left, or the right, or somewhere else, and retrieve the reprint in question, turn to page 19, and lo and behold, there indeed was the article in question. The man had a freakish, photographic memory.

Klixbull's (we had got onto Christian names by this time) secretary came in after a while carrying two cups of black tea. I was not asked if I would like milk. The monologue continued, the great man never flagging for a moment. At one time, I got the opportunity to quiz my host a little about his time in Copenhagen, being careful, and polite, to omit all mention of Carl Ballhausen. Later, somehow, the conversation turned to languages and I asked Klixbull which languages he spoke. Jørgensen replied, without any sense of conceit or even pride really, that he spoke Danish of course — his native tongue — English, French, German, Icelandic (I supposed that that was fairly close to Danish), Greek, Mandarin, Italian and probably a couple of others too. Mind you, I don't know whether his mastery of all those tongues was equally peculiar; his English was a splendidly amusing travesty of the real thing. Even so... Jørgensen went on to tell me that he regretted not having yet mastered Spanish. It was some time much later in the afternoon, that he took me to an hotel where he thanked me for my lecture and abruptly said goodbye. That was the end of my visit to the University of Geneva. I don't accuse Jørgensen of being rude. This senior figure had devoted several hours of his time to his dissenting visitor, after all. He was just an odd man and there are many of those around academe.

I went out for dinner, strolling into what seemed to me to be a popular tourists' eating district. Suddenly, I saw a sign offering fondue. Then I saw dozens of them. I had forgotten about this famous Swiss dish but then remembered having eaten one in Geneva many years earlier. I chose a restaurant, more or less at random, and ordered a plain fondue and a bottle of rosé. While waiting for my meal to arrive, I looked around the place. I was impressed with its homely atmosphere and... then I suddenly realised that this was the exact same restaurant I had enjoyed all that time ago. It seems that, in this limited example anyway, my taste has been constant. Once more, I enjoyed the fondue and my bottle and when I finally retired to bed, I was a happy bunny again.

Next morning, I caught the train to Basel. The French call it Basle (pronounced *Bâle*) but the locals identify with the German-speaking part of Switzerland (although they tend to speak Swiss-German or *Schweizerdeutsch* amongst themselves). My reason for this visit was totally personal. I had given a lecture at the University of Basel in the past but on this occasion my excuse to return to this most interesting city was to touch base once more with old friends and colleagues from Cambridge.

Edwin and Catherine Constable had been chemistry lecturers there when they got married; later, they moved to the University of Basel to a pair of professorships. That's quite a difficult manoeuvre because two chairs in the same subject rarely come up or, as in their case, are created especially for a married couple. It says a lot about the esteem in which they were held. Apart from their professional devotion to chemistry, Ed and Cathy love food and travel, and Basel is more or less at a geographical focal point of four cultures — French, German, Italian and Swiss. The city is geographically half in Switzerland and half in Germany. All that in addition to those characteristics belonging uniquely to the Swiss. It depends on which direction you choose to travel a few kilometres as to which cuisine and culture you will encounter. They revelled in all this and shared their enthusiasm with me — and Gwyn, when she had accompanied me on a couple of occasions.

One small event is worth recording on this particular visit was when I had been taken out and about in Basel and after morning coffee, Ed had suggested that we cross the

River Rhine which flows through the middle of the city and which is quite wide there. His reason wasn't really to take me into the German part of the city, but simply to show me a famous mechanism for crossing a river, namely the "reaction ferry". The ferry itself is simply a pontoon which is loosely tethered to an overhead cable (the cable is in the water for some reaction ferries elsewhere in the world) and a strong rudder. The pontoon moves across the river, as if "tacking", under the force of the water flow while the tethering cable, which boasts a loop at its top end, slips along the overhead guide cable. A yacht tacks against the wind; a reaction ferry sort of tacks against the water. No engines of any kind are involved. The stronger the flow, the faster the ferry moves, and the Rhine is quite powerful through Basel. We crossed the river and so found ourselves in Germany, but since there were other things Ed had planned for the rest of my short visit, we immediately returned to Switzerland.

Back onto the train the following day, and so on to Strasbourg, which is only an hour north of Basel. I was scheduled to give a lecture in the university there. On arrival in Strasbourg, I caught a cab to the hotel in which a room had been booked for me. It was clean and pleasant though a longish walk into the city centre, not that I minded, for, after settling in, I took myself off to explore the place a bit.

Yet again, it is a beautiful city. It has only about a quarter of a million residents in the central part, though many more in what may be called Greater Strasbourg. It lies today within the French border with Germany and is the capital of the region called Alsace. That region has been part of Germany from time to time, and as Schleswig-Holstein in the Baltic region of Germany has a history of being part of Denmark or Germany depending upon the day of the week, the Alsace region has been claimed by both France and Germany several times. Hopefully, things are more settled these days. Strasbourg (*Strassburg* in German) is the formal seat of the European Parliament these days, of course, so that many shiny new buildings have appeared outside of the old, central area.

By the way, Strasbourg is very old indeed, being founded in 12BC as a Roman camp. I found a small café for lunch before taking himself off on one of my "random walks". I was picked up at my hotel in the evening to be taken to dinner by a man I had wanted to meet for a long time. John Osborn had been a postgraduate of the man who lectured to me as professor of inorganic chemistry at Imperial College in London where I had been both undergraduate and graduate, Geoffrey Wilkinson.

Wilkinson had been anything but like the conventional image of a university professor. He hailed from the north of England but having spent considerable time in the United States, had picked up a sort of American accent. It was a poor effort, though, and to my ears at least, he always sounded rather comical. More than that, however, was his habit of sniffing out, rather than in — which, by the way, is quite difficult to imitate… er cleanly, shall we say — at a rate which was directly in proportion to his excitement. I recall sitting next to him at a lecture in the front row, as professors almost invariably do, sniffing at a constant but slow rate when the lecturer's material turned to some of Wilkinson's own work. There was no criticism of Wilkinson's work involved, rather the contrary, but as his name was mentioned, his rate of sniffing increased ten-fold. I am convinced that Wilkinson's habit was nothing more than a nervous tic; that he was still unsure of himself even after the considerable success he had had at that stage in his career.

That success was to blossom in spades a few years after that incident, when Geoff, as he was affectionately known to almost all who knew him, was awarded a Nobel Prize for his work in synthetic chemistry. I was but one of very many chemists who liked and admired Geoffrey Wilkinson enormously.

My host for dinner that evening in Strasbourg had worked very closely with Geoff, was a good friend of his, and in part but deservedly, owed his professorship in Strasbourg to his former boss. I had not met John before that evening but was a close friend of another research student of Wilkinson who knew and admired John very much, both as a chemist and personally. So I was really curious to meet my host for the evening.

John Osborn was several years older than me and had been in that Strasbourg chair for several years by that time. He turned out to be every bit as pleasant a guy as I had been led to believe but also considerably more sophisticated than me, something to which my antennae have always been tuned — maybe hyper-tuned — to all my life, from primary school to Cambridge don. In part, John's social superiority stemmed equally, I guessed, from his intrinsic intelligence and current seniority, as from his years in this most sophisticated of environments. Being bilingual here was common, even essential. So also, really, was being trilingual, if that third language was (universal) English, as was John. Such was the nature of the place. In Basel, Ed had soon acquired a good, working knowledge of French, German and even of Schweizerdeutsch, the latter being an imperative in his later position as head of department even though it had little relevance outside of that corner of Switzerland.

I have always admired linguistic ability but have never shown any flair for it. Mind you, I have never really had the need for it. As I have pointed out many times, my focus in those days was extremely narrow. I knew my business all right but rarely strayed from it. Anyway, I had a most enjoyable evening with the affable John Osborn, who returned me to my hotel afterwards.

I simply must tell you of another memory of my time in Strasbourg which must be worth repeating, surely. Maybe not. You decide, dear reader!

Like many others, I'm sure, I have noticed how French design can be — how shall I say? — quirky. Think of Citroen cars, for example, or of the Art Nouveau subway station entrances in Paris. Well, the same goes for French toilets. On several occasions in my travels, I have come across a public toilet — public in the sense that it was on offer in some restaurant where I was eating — in which a square porcelain base with slightly elevated foot shapes moulded therein was overhung with a showerhead. Apparently, the idea was to assume a crouching position with your feet on the "plinths" provided and to use the shower afterwards to wash the result away.

Well, the toilet in my hotel wasn't as crude as that; indeed, it was clearly spanking new, expensive, and of the "latest design". There was no seat, you were to sit upon the bare rim — itself a somewhat uncomfortable experience — and so, at least, be more or less at one with the rest of the civilised world, but your shit was not deposited into water, whose greatest boon, if you think about it, is to submerge the stink, but rather onto a flat, elevated porcelain area only inches below your bum. Afterwards, the toilet flush came from the front of the toilet, spraying backwards with such force that the mess is washed away completely and nearly instantaneously. Even given that these last two attributes were a considerable success, the smell in your nostrils meanwhile was really disgusting. As I say, French design can be quirky. Thinking about it now, I wonder if it was some kind of "medical" toilet whose design allowed one to examine or sample your faeces before they are immersed in water; if so, why have one in a hotel? And by the way, there wasn't another, more conventional toilet on offer in the room. I just couldn't resist telling you about this in detail — front to rear, you might say.

Next morning, John met me at the hotel to take me off to meet his colleagues and research group. John's speciality was close to Wilkinson's, which was hardly surprising, but therefore considerably removed from my theoretical area. John's researchers were all enthusiastic and very clearly adored their boss, something I always like to see. I mainly listened as they each took turns in an informal way to tell me about their individual work while everyone sipped a morning coffee.

In due course, it was time for my lecture, and as ever in departments which specialised in synthetic work, I expected to receive little more than a polite response from my audience. That was not the case in Strasbourg. Several members of the audience made good suggestions and asked interesting and interested questions and I realised that members of theoretical groups were also present. In many ways, my work was such that I fell between two stools being equally "rejected" by synthetic inorganic chemists and by so-called "physical/theoretical" chemists. In a way, my work straddled aspects of traditional inorganic chemistry and physics. Often, therefore, I had to think fast and work hard to keep my end up. I had grown ever more used to defending my work under such circumstances, but nevertheless, it could be taxing.

For the most part, however, things went well but then I got eyed by one member of the audience, clearly someone senior like myself, who decided to "have a go" at me. As I heard the Australian twang of my questioner, I realised who was asking the question. I had heard of Dick Field (not his real name, by the way) from various sources over the years, and indeed, had consulted his work from time to time. I had been told how sharp Field was and I concentrated hard on what he had to say. His observation was more of a challenge than a question. It was something of an attack, and a few years earlier, I would have stumbled or even wilted before it. Actually, it was a rude thing to do to a visiting lecturer for the questioner was simply focussed on his own self-aggrandisement. However, by this time in my career, I felt more than able to gobble up this little twerp. However, I proceeded cautiously and politely, but Dick Field kept at it in an increasingly hostile fashion. I waited for a moment when Field had exaggerated his point too much and then firmly, but politely, put him in his place in such a way that everybody in the lecture theatre understood; including Field himself who, to be fair, shut up immediately. Judging by some of the glances going round the room, I felt that I had not only succeeded in making my point but that there were people around who were only too happy to see Field get his. It seems, I learned some while afterwards, that Field pulled this trick on many visitors and often won. But not that day.

When the dust had settled on my lecture and all questions had been discussed, and hopefully, answered, I was taken along to see the current head of department (a circulating appointment amongst the most senior academics in that department), a Frenchman by the name of Jean-Marie Lehn. We got no further than a handshake and me being seated, before Lehn's phone rang, and with a gesture of apology, the boss answered it. There followed a long conversation in French — about what I had absolutely no idea, of course — a conversation which switched between French and German with no apparent break whatsoever. Once more, I was mesmerised by such facility. In due course, that all came to an end and with another apology, Lehn asked me, in English now, about my trip so far, where I had been, where I would be, and so on. Lehn's reputation was known to me, especially from my mate, Ed in Basel. It was a very fine reputation indeed and the man was regarded as some sort of demigod in Strasbourg. He spent a few minutes telling me about his own work which I thought more than polite given my own interests were so different.

Some months later, by the way, I suffered the nearest thing to a heart attack I had ever experienced when I received in my mailbox at my lab back in Cambridge, a letter from the Swedish Academy of Sciences. It was printed on the finest of paper in a delightful font. It asked me (and, I soon realised, hundreds of other scientists around the world) if I would like to nominate anyone for a Nobel Prize. Oh well… I thought. I found it interesting, however, that it was only upon being officially asked for my opinion that I actually gave the matter really serious thought instead of the usual flippancy of the coffee room. I sent off just one name — Jean-Marie Lehn. It turned out that Lehn got the Prize that very year. I was ever so pleased, if only because my judgement coincided with that of so many others.

I have heard people say of such-and-such a Nobel laureate, that he or she didn't deserve the award. I insist that such is a misbegotten view, for a winner is only so decided after canvassing views from probably hundreds of his or her fellows, such remarks are as much an insult to the community as to the recipient. But there could be exceptions… Anyway, fine though Lehn's reputation was when I gave my lecture in Strasbourg, the Nobel Prize had not yet been conferred upon my host.

I met him again several years later, incidentally and informally, in Australia as well as having heard him lecture once in Cambridge. As I have said already, my interests were in a different area, yet I sat in that audience for nigh on two hours — twice the normal length of a seminar — without a single ache or desire for the lecture to end. It's not fair, is it, how some people are gifted with so much. I refer, too, at this point, to the fact, told me by one of my colleagues in the university world, that Lehn was also a fine pianist. He had been trained to concert level and would often respond to calls for a performance at chemistry conferences after dinner where a piano had been laid on with malice aforethought, as it were, when, without music, he would launch into any one of dozens of the classics in the repertoire. Makes you weep!

Enough of this hero-worship! Our story must go on and we take it up as I reached my next port of call — Braunschweig once again.

8

Rudolf Krause had attended a chemistry conference in Cambridge about six months earlier. As you know by now, his speciality had nothing in common with mine, but I knew of Rudolf's presence around the place and made a point of inviting him to join Gwyn and me at our cottage for dinner one evening; indeed, I picked him up from his conference venue and later deposited him at the college where he was billeted. We often entertained visiting academics in our home, either because I wanted to return hospitality as now, or because I knew there might well come a time when I visited this guest; or sometimes, simply as our contribution to the world-wide network of academic visiting rites. It's a fairly common practice in academic circles although some of my colleagues felt the need rather less than we did.

Gwyn had cooked something quite special for our guest and we had opened a nice bottle to warm the evening. Rudolf was polite and grateful as a guest, but he was hard work. Jack had told me a long time ago that Krause was an anglophile and that certainly came through during the evening but somehow, he didn't seem to relax.

Gwyn's memory of our evening is overwhelmingly of a hypochondriac. Rudolf kept mentioning his heart and how he took pills every day. Well, maybe he has a problem there, I had argued, but I had to concede that our guest did keep on about it. But it wasn't just his heart. It seems there was something wrong with his wrist, with his stomach, and God knows what else. Rudolf never smiled and mostly spoke in a quiet monotone; steady rather than measured, tones. At one point in our conversation, I reminded Krause of our visiting the fence between the two halves of Germany. I again expressed my gratitude for having been shown that disgusting construction, and my horror at what we had seen. Rudolf shrugged and said it was something they had to live with. When pushed a little, he went on to acknowledge that he would visit friends in the East, and a couple of old relatives, every other month. When I asked if he felt nervous on those trips, Rudolf admitted to some degree of worry but not too much. Altogether, it was difficult getting to grips with this conversation. Anyway, some months after that conference, Rudolf had written to me, thanked me for a delightful evening and suggested that I visit Braunschweig again sometime. So here I was. Just for a couple of nights and this time, I had no plans to give a lecture. This was purely social.

Krause met me at the station in the late afternoon and took me to his home on this occasion rather than a hotel, as I would have preferred. But this was my host saying thank you for looking after him in Cambridge. One plus point, certainly, was that I got to meet Rudolf's wife, Christa, who was as open as her husband was not. It was, of course, merely a matter of personality and I understood this perfectly. I was allocated what had been one of their sons' bedroom, he having fled the nest some years earlier, and advised to come down as soon as convenient for a tipple or two before dinner.

We spent a happy hour chatting about the Krauses' trips around the world and comparing notes with those Gwyn and I had taken together. The German couple obviously went in for physical exercise, hill climbing, cycling and so on, which the Gerlochs have always indulged, if at all, by way of the television set. I was used to meeting people like this. I used to feel inadequate and trivial in their company, but as the years go by, have discovered that I can take it on the chin without a whiff of guilt. Christa had cooked a schnitzel for dinner which was more than acceptable. Our conversations went far into the evening before I excused myself and went to bed.

Before going to sleep, however, I had a look at the books on the many shelves around the room. Actually, there were very few books. Instead, the shelves were packed to the gunwales with magazines. I took one out at random and opened it. It was filled with train timetables. Nothing else, apart from the routes and the year — or half-year, as appropriate. If that were not surprising enough, I soon found that they were not simply devoted to the German rail system but included the French, British and even some American lines as well. I was most careful to replace the magazines I glanced at, very carefully into their proper places, for it was obvious that this was the collection of a fanatic. I remembered how my friend, Carl Ballhausen, professor of theoretical chemistry at the Ørsted Institute in Copenhagen, had a phrase for this kind of thing, 'A man must have an occupation!' he would drawl, with a mile-wide grin across his face. Then I felt a little guilty for, truth to tell, few of my friends and colleagues were free of what others might have regarded as nutty hobbies. Maybe I wasn't free of them myself?

Next morning, over breakfast, I mentioned that I had found the magazines. Rudolf wasn't fazed one little bit but jumped straight into a long exposition on his favourite subject, admitting that he didn't collect these timetables for utilitarian purposes but rather in the spirit of the trainspotter. I remembered standing on a street in Hull as a kid, recording car numberplates in a small notebook, but I had very soon become tired of the whole thing. I said nothing about that, however, but surreptitiously glanced at Christa. She was careful not to make a thing of it, but her return glance made clear her own disinterest in the whole enterprise. When our meal was finished, Rudolf announced that he would take me on a car ride into East Germany.

'Of course!' I exclaimed. 'The Berlin Wall came down last year. I cried when that happened.'

'And the rest of the partition between the Germanys came down, or was breached, only a couple of months ago,' Rudolf informed me. 'Would you like to go?'

It was a marvellous opportunity to see the other side while still "hot", as it were, and I enthusiastically assented.

'We'll take some sandwiches with us for lunch,' my host said, the first hint I had of the amount of time this trip was to take.

As on my last trip to the fence, our journey took us about half an hour to the border. I had expected that we would cross by the Helmstedt-Marienborn border crossing where I had cheekily sneered at a GDR guard with binoculars. We could have done, Rudolf explained, but now that the border no longer legally existed, there were several more convenient places where we could cross. Much of the fence with its tank trap and double razor wire was still in place. After all, you cannot demolish hundreds of kilometres of that kind of thing in mere months. But where old country roads had once come to an abrupt halt at the wire, the barrier had been removed and the road opened so that pre-war — or perhaps I should say pre-communist — maps became relevant once more.

However, as we drove across the defunct border, the road quality deteriorated markedly and instantly. The smooth West German road surface was replaced abruptly by very many, seriously dangerous potholes and Rudolf had to slow down and keep a sharp lookout. I assumed that the road condition would improve once we reached a road which had not simply been aligned towards the old fence, but I soon discovered that not to be so. We drove for miles around the countryside as Krause took me from one village to another, but all the roads were in equally stark disrepair. It was going to cost millions to put all this right, I thought.

At first, my attention to the villages we drove through was rather casual. I saw old settlements, much as you might find on a similar drive in many parts of Britain, albeit with different architecture, and I was aware that they were somewhat dilapidated. Just how dilapidated, however, only became apparent when Rudolf pulled up next to one old stone wall, a wall which was part of an old house or cottage. Or rather, it had been part of an old building, for now it was part of a ruin. Krause pointed to the guttering at the top of the wall. It had rusted completely away in one part and not been repaired. As a result, after a few years of neglect, the guttering section had collapsed, rainwater had flowed into the stone wall, and most significantly, into the mortar. The mortar had slowly weakened, grass or such had taken root there, and under that simple organic pressure, some stonework had then collapsed, only to expose the wall to the elements even more. And so on. I understood completely for I'd long been a bit of a geek so far as building methods are concerned, but was, nevertheless, amazed that only one or two decades of neglect could wreak such damage to so solid a structure. I began to look at other buildings in the area only to find the story repeated everywhere. It was terrible, but when Rudolf told me that the East German communists — likely under directions from the Russians — had neglected these buildings *deliberately*, I was disgusted. The Russian post-war punishment of the Germans for their callous invasion of *their* homeland during the war was, it seems, never-ending. Did the Germans deserve such treatment, I wondered? If so, that can go on for ever, surely, and other wars will surely follow. After all, that had already happened within that very century already. My mood was becoming ever more sombre as the day wore on.

We drove to yet another village and I was beginning to wonder why Krause was so keen to show me repeat performances, as it were, for the point had been surely made by now. But there was more to Rudolf's tale. This time, we drove, slowly as ever, to the central square in the place. The village was, again, quite small and its central meeting place was to scale. Sited around the square were several old, two- and three-storey, stone buildings but here there were signs of maintenance and repair, and of occupation. I guessed that the four sides of the square had been filled with such houses at some earlier time but now, anyway, there were three or four large irregular-sized gaps between those houses which remained standing.

Those gaps had been filled with modern, concrete, seven- and eight-storey blocks of flats in the clearest of Russian communist style. These buildings were merely blocks of concrete with small windows arranged in straight lines with no thought for proportion or subtlety. One might complain about some of the concrete monstrosities built in post-war Britain, but they would be awarded a Nobel Prize for architecture in comparison with these insults to humanity. Not only were these buildings aesthetically obnoxious, they were insultingly out of scale. They should never have been built next to a village square. Even worse, if such were possible, they were built cheek-by-jowl with the stone houses which had been there, possibly for centuries, I mean, within *centimetres* of them. They were the architectural equivalent of thumping some poor fight victim and then rubbing his bloodied nose into the ground.

'That's enough,' was all that I could say. Rudolf said nothing and we slowly drove off along a country road where the communists had had no control of Nature's weeds and trees. We stopped and began to eat our sandwiches. We had been touring around The East for about two hours. I thought that we'd be making our way back home after our lunch, but Krause had yet more to do and show.

'I want to do a bit of shopping while we're here,' he said. What could he possibly find worth having here? I thought. Rudolf continued, 'I want to buy a few groceries.'

Groceries then in the East could hardly compare with those in the West, I thought but held my tongue. We drove for another quarter of an hour — to a small town this time. Once more, there were many old stone buildings but now, possibly because of a different construction style, there were few signs of decay. We pulled up in a central square which actually wasn't square but rather five-sided in an irregular fashion and with a high stone wall along one side. Built into this stone wall were several small shops and Krause led us to one of them. It was a grocery shop in the old style. I offered to stay in the car, but he insisted that I accompany him so that he could introduce me to the owner.

I had been in such places back home when I was a kid. You know, the sort of place with a counter and where sugar was sold by the half pound, collected with a large scoop from a big bin behind the counter, and packaged in a blue paper bag whose top was folded in a miraculous manner to seal the contents. It brought childhood memories flooding back to me. By the late 1980s, however, such memories were quaint at best and nobody in their right mind today would contemplate buying their stuff like that. Rudolf spoke quietly to the shop keeper and her assistant for quite a long time, and in due course, led me out of the shop while he carried a string bag filled to the brim with various everyday items for Christa's pantry.

As we drove off, Rudolf explained that he liked to go to the East now once a week to buy such groceries. He acknowledged that they cost considerably more than he would pay in a West German supermarket, but he liked to make his small contribution to the welfare of his unfortunate East German fellows. I thought that it was a very fine gesture. And that was the end of our tour that day; we turned for home, saying little as the road returned from potholes to smooth tarmac and a fast ride home.

It was clear that Christa knew exactly how our day had gone. It was equally clear that she had accompanied Rudolf on such trips herself. She also understood my initial silence about it; maybe only partly understood, because I myself didn't come to terms with the day completely until a long while later. She presented us with a pleasant meal once more, and after a little lubrication, conversation began to take place. I did try to detail my feelings about various parts of the trip, and it was clear they understood. We never, however, got anywhere near to discussing the war.

I departed from the Krauses after breakfast next day, taking the slow train for the short trip to Hanover where I changed onto an express train (not an ICE superfast train on this occasion) for my longish journey west, I had about half an hour to wait for the second leg. My next venue was to be Nijmegen in The Netherlands, the first of two universities in which I had planned to lecture in that country. The journey would take some six hours to Arnhem where I was to be met.

The carriage in which I sat was one of those which are divided into compartments rather than the more common open-plan layout of more recent times. I shared the compartment with just two other passengers for most of the journey.

At first, I amused myself by looking at the scenery through which we sped but began to feel somewhat listless as I ruminated about my visit to the East. No thoughts crystalised clearly at first but as time went by, I began to see the events of this trip to Braunschweig melded with those of my visit a couple of years earlier. A mist of confusion and discomfort began to form. I looked at my travelling companions, two obviously German men, who seemed to be a little too uptight and proper for my taste. I hadn't really noticed fellow passengers on other segments of my train journey through Europe this time or the last, so why should I be so aware of them now? But I was, and as time rolled by, I became more so.

Were they watching me? I felt sure that I'd seen the odd sideways glance in my direction. I turned my head a little to look more closely at my companions and to make it obvious that I was doing so but it evoked no response as far as I could see. My anxiety slowly but inexorably increased as the hours passed, and by the time we were approaching Dortmund, I was sitting bolt upright and very stiffly in my seat, sure that the older chap in the corner seat was watching me intently. However, the man left the compartment at Dortmund and I, as casually as I was able, moved into the corridor to check whether my watcher had left the train. He had and I even watched him leave the station on the far side. Feeling rather silly, I regained my seat as the train left the station. But I still felt very nervous. This is so stupid, I thought, I've never felt like this before. My thoughts began to oscillate wildly from one viewpoint to another.

After some time — I would guess after another hour — I became convinced that my discomfort was directly associated with the country I was travelling in, with Germany. I was born in 1939, a month or so before World War II broke out or, if you prefer, before the Germans invaded Poland. As a baby and then a small child in Hull, I had almost no memories of the war. Hull was bombed very heavily in the early stages of the war because of its importance as Britain's third port, but the bombardment lasted for only three days, and as far as I knew, wasn't repeated.

I do remember a window in the back room of our family home being blown in and some years later, when I talked about this recollection, my parents agreed that it had happened and that the bomb responsible had landed in a field about a kilometre away. Why drop a bomb in a field? Almost certainly, it wasn't a mistake but merely a German bomber not wishing to return home with any unused bombs on board the aircraft, so it just dumped them randomly as it turned for home.

Most homes in Hull had been provided with a thick, concrete air-raid shelter. Many were Anderson shelters but others, like ours were cubical in shape. I never knew the pros and cons of the two designs, although I learned many years later that the Anderson shelters were given free to those with an income less than five pounds per week. I knew that our shelter came with the house when my parents bought it new just as the war began. It was, by the way, a very pleasant house but modest. I do recall spending a miserable couple of hours — or so it seemed to me — in that shelter with my parents on just two occasions throughout the whole war. It was cold and dank in there. As I said, Hull was bombed just once. I lost no relatives in the war, to bombs, bullets or accidents.

My father was a nominal Catholic; nominal because, although he was baptised as such, he had never, in his adult life, knowingly attended any service, and because of what he perceived as the grasping nature of some nuns who regularly came with their begging bowl to his parents, who were as poor as church mice. Rightly or wrongly, he had developed a strong disgust for the Church and for religion in general.

My mother was a Jew; a Jew who had married out, much to the great distress and even anger of at least (most?) one of her many siblings. She was not the only one of the children to marry out, but she copped the worst flack, probably because she was the oldest girl and because she had assumed the position of *quasi* mother to her younger brothers and sisters after their mother died rather young. My mum cared strongly about her Jewish heritage — about her race, if you like — but not particularly about her religion.

My parents, therefore, shared a common distrust, or worse, for religion in general. When I came along — and I remained an "only child" — they had me baptised into the Church of England, simply because that seemed the sort of thing one did in England in those days and in that place. When the time came to choose a school for me, they chose a

Church of England school for the simple reason that it was the closest school to our home and because I would be able to walk to it safely without crossing any main roads. Remember this was in 1950 when traffic was light, and in any case, we didn't possess a car; and more, parents simply didn't drive their children to school then, even if they were rich enough to do so.

I had discussed my mother's formal faith and race with her on several occasions, but she had never pushed me in any direction except by example; that is away from religion. She had, of course, told me years ago that, being the child of a Jewish mother, with emphasis on the mother, I was automatically a Jew myself. I never underwent the bar mitzvah ceremony, however. I "got religion" (Christian) in my thirteenth year and my parents quietly smiled indulgently. I shed this fad after three intense weeks. The sickness never returned. My agnosticism grew over the years until I felt sufficiently confident to claim myself as an atheist and brush off accusations of childish certainty.

In the fifties and later, I saw several war films, and later, documentaries about the war. The portrayal of Germans as callous brutes was common in these films, mostly because their plots centred on the Gestapo. But even regular war scenes of soldiers bursting into the homes of civilians of the occupied nation, throwing someone out of their home, or simply destroying their home and/or possessions always moved me to anger. To be fair, I felt the same if it were the "good guys" who did these things, but such instances were few and far between in the films I had seen.

Physical harm to any person or animal has always been something of intense horror to me; I feel much the same about violence towards their possessions. So, because of the (naturally) unbalanced sampling of such war films, I, no doubt along with thousands of other Britons, French, Poles, Greeks, Russians and the rest, had developed a suspicion of, a nervousness towards, Germans. Surely such is just a typical tale of those who have seen, or just heard about, any war throughout time. However, whether it is right or wrong, or wrong-headed, it is surely understandable and natural.

A further layer of confusion here may be the fact that my father's mother was Bavarian — as I mentioned earlier — but also that his grandfather was either Danish or German, coming as he did from Schleswig-Holstein. I never heard Dad make pro-German remarks throughout his whole life; if anything, such references were more likely to be anti-German but in respect of what he saw as their clumsiness and heavy-handed approach to life.

Amongst the documentaries, and then films, which I have seen over the years have been accounts of Auschwitz, Belsen and the rest of those atrocities. I had come to learn of Hitler's great hatred of the Jews and learned that it was a sentiment shared by very many Germans though, most emphatically, not all Germans. Like any half-decent, sentient person, I had been more horrified than I could say about what had happened in those concentration camps. I didn't just feel blazing anger but outright nausea and incomprehension that human beings of one belief could do such things to human beings of another.

By the way, it was many years later before I began to ask the questions. How long has antisemitism been going on? How widespread has it been? Does it exist in Britain? All obvious questions, of course, but I hadn't asked them. Why not? Because, I think, I hadn't come across any antisemitism personally. The concept was just that to me, a concept. As I have remarked several times already, I learned about life mostly from experience because, I suppose, I didn't read much. In writing this story, I have been tempted to disguise this fact — for it isn't something to be proud of — but it is a fact, and I believe, one shared by many. In retirement, I have begun to read biographies, often political ones; novels by British, French and Russian novelists of the nineteenth century; and by German and American ones from the twentieth century. My eyes have widened as I repeatedly read about strongly antisemitic views throughout that literature. Hitler's thugs hadn't invented the idea. It has been around for a long time.

When did it begin? Well, I presume since the time of Christ because "the Jews killed Christ". And of course, because so many Jews were so savvy so far as making a buck out of usuary — as those who had no money and expected others to make loans to them for nothing called it. What about Shakespeare's story of Shylock, for example?

The point for us here, for me on that train heading west out of Germany in the '80s, was that I had been exposed to all manner of images and ideas which might have been designed to make me distrust or even hate Germans. I didn't believe that I hated them, but I did believe that I was scared of them. I believed in a "them". Being a reasonable, intelligent and enquiring sort of man, I sought to find the origins of the thoughts I was experiencing then and there. I remembered those post-docs in Braunschweig who had entertained me on my first trip to that place. 'Vee have the same sense of chooma,' and all that. 'Let us Chermans and you Pritish get together and beat the shit out of the others,' or words to that effect, in 1936 — four years before I was born. It was I who had made that connection, for God's sake, not my young hosts who were only trying to be pleasant. I had lost no relatives or friends in the war, or as a direct result of it, so far as I was aware. In particular, my mother's Jewish family had lost nobody in the war, in a concentration camp, or even under an allied bomb. Her family had left the Baltic States in the first few years of the twentieth century, way before Hitler came on the scene. Mind you, it was the turn of the Russians to persecute the Jews on that occasion, was it not? I wasn't personally involved in all that, however. I don't say that as some way to excuse myself from something. I am simply stating a fact.

Years later, in a discussion with a good Jewish friend of mine, Peter Holland, of whom I am very fond, the son of a Jewish father and Jewish mother, whose family, at the proximity of uncles and aunts, I think, had lost many family members in the Holocaust, I pointed out that I was born in 1939 and was barely socially conscious before 1950 (which in my case was pushing it a bit), and horrified though I was by what the Nazis had done, saw no reason to feel any guilt myself. My friend replied with obviously heart-felt sincerity,

'We are all guilty.' I have struggled for years with that remark and even now, only dimly comprehend the deep truth in it.

Anyway, during that journey through Germany, my feelings about the Holocaust were of utter horror but not of *personal* loss. Even so, after all I had seen of what the communists had done in the GDR, I could feel sympathy for those East Germans who had been imprisoned in their own country by the Russians. And of course, by those of their fellows who had sought to improve their own lot at the immense expense of most other East Germans. I mean, the Stasi were utter pigs. Then again, there must have been many Germans living close to those Nazi deathcamps in the war, people who must have either known about, or had undeniable suspicions of, what their fellow Germans were doing. Yes, Germany does bear a degree of guilt for those members of its society, I reasoned, and concluded that that was, in part at least, responsible for my discomfort on that journey. And then, was the remaining companion in my compartment some sort of Stasi spy, surreptitiously watching what this inquisitive Britisher had been doing in the former GDR? Well, that particular companion left the train in Essen a short distance further on. I checked that out as well.

What are the origins of prejudice? Mostly, I guess, ignorance and the fear that accompanies it. In the present context, as I got to meet and to know individual Germans, I found that I liked them, disliked them, or didn't quite know yet, in just the same sort of way I would respond to people of any other nation that I had met. The senior tutor for much of my time in Trinity Hall, Ernest Frankl, and his wife, Carmen, were German. They had left — fled — Germany in 1931, I think, seeing the writing on the wall so far as their home country was concerned, and made their new home in England. They shared so many admirable qualities. Ernest was as astute as they come and this was coupled with a worldly-wise patience which made him, by pretty common consent, the best senior tutor in Cambridge at that time. A senior tutor's job is to oversee the lives of all students in his college and to drench any fires which might suddenly arise. Ernest was one of our college's greatest assets. In many ways, he ran the place. Carmen was a delightful person, something of an artist, a generous hostess, and a companion for her husband, the like of whom I have never met before or since in my life. How could I not like and admire so wonderful a couple? However, as usual, I must muddy the waters. They spoke English with absolutely no trace of a German accent (I heard that Ernest refused to speak his native tongue after coming to England); indeed, their English accents were somewhat aristocratic. So obviously, that made them so much easier to like! There we go again, prejudice.

On the other hand, I remember a sort of mate of mine, a fellow undergraduate at Imperial College in London, György Horvarth, who so impressed me in my deep well of gaucherie when I entered that college, fresh from school in Hull. György taught me about coffee, including an assertion that the strongest coffee in the world was not Turkish but Hungarian. When I asked how that worked out, he explained that Hungarians would eat bread and butter spread with coffee grounds. In my naïvety, I swallowed that line, grounds and all, for all of five minutes. György was far more worldly than me. I knew it and admired him greatly for it. I immediately assumed that all continentals were thus. I also had absolutely no problem with his very strong, albeit rather mellifluous, accent. He came into college every day, wearing a smart suit (as an undergraduate, I remind you; 1959 or not), carrying, and swinging, a tightly furled umbrella. Such sophistication! Since that day, I have been convinced that all Hungarians are sophisticates. Since that day, I have held all Hungarians in high esteem. Okay, so I'm an impressionable idiot to think that György could be an avatar for all his countrymen. Nobody else makes that kind of mistake, do they?

What was I saying earlier? Ah yes, prejudice derives from ignorance. And I'll add to that, an ability to analyse one's thoughts about such things only develops with experience. How often have I written that, expert on such world-stopping, important matters as ligand-field theory and magnetochemistry as I was, my experience of Life was surely delicate. Well now, let's get back to that train journey.

A couple of hours later, an announcement came over the intercom in three languages — German, French and Dutch. The message was clear, we had just crossed the border into The Netherlands. I, as the now solitary passenger in that compartment, breathed a heartfelt sigh of relief. I don't mean this in any figurative way, there was no acting as my spine curled a little and I relaxed into my seat. I couldn't help myself as I experienced an enormous sense of joy. I had visited friends and colleagues in The Netherlands before and

I knew I would be safe and happy now. Meanwhile, I realised, I had discovered that I had been deeply unhappy about being in Germany.

9

I alighted at Arnhem in fading light where an academic chemist from the University of Nijmegen met me. We had never met before, and by prior arrangement, I again carried one of my books under my arm. I had written it a few years earlier, but its limited sales suggested that either it was no good, which I fervently did not believe, or that its subject was a minority sport. That was surely right, wasn't it?

My host was a pleasant young man, who I shall call Daan Visser. It's not his real name, nor that of Eva, his wife, for reasons which will become obvious. I guessed that he had been a lecturer for a short time only. Daan drove me to his home in Nijmegen which is only about twenty-five kilometres away. The arrangement, which had been settled before I left Cambridge, was that I would spend just one night in Nijmegen, staying at Daan's home, which was a most generous gesture under the circumstances.

Daan introduced his wife who showed me to my room which, though quite small, as are so many Dutch houses and rooms, was very cosy, welcoming and warm. Then began one of the more memorable meals of my life. All three of us sat around a coffee table upon which were three tumblers and one small sherry glass. Daan explained that he and Eva were teetotal and would drink a glass of lemonade to welcome their guest, but if I preferred, a glass of sherry was available. I chose the sherry and realised almost immediately that that was a big mistake, it was cooking sherry. Ah well, at least I was feeling so much more relaxed now than I had all day, and it was clear that my hosts, gauche though they may be, were genuinely trying to be welcoming and were nice people.

I cottoned on now to the fact that Daan's university had no entertainment funds available. I had come across this problem before but not for a long time. Anyway, that was why I had not been found a hotel room for the night. As I have said, Gwyn and I often had visiting academics to the University of Cambridge, despite its normally looking after visitors, over for dinner in our cottage, but that was our choice and when we did that, we served up a splendid meal and oceans of good booze. What decadent people!

Daan and Eva were very young in the scheme of things and clearly had no background in the debauched ways in which my friends and I revelled. So we sat there and chatted about the places I had been to and what I thought of them. I studiously avoided any discussion about my feelings about Germany, lest my hosts think me a xenophobe, something I doubted myself but was struggling with inside, nevertheless. We didn't talk about work because Eva had no connection to the university beyond being Daan's wife. Conversation didn't flag, however, and continued happily over the dinner to follow.

Daan invited me to sit at their dinner table, which was laid with water tumblers, this time being no surprise to me.

Eva brought in a very large bowl which is worth describing in detail. It was about twenty centimetres high, twenty-five centimetres in diameter at the top but far narrower at the bottom. I guess it was the same shape as a common or garden cooking bowl but larger and made of ceramic rather than glass. It was full almost to the brim with a very dark-green-leaved vegetable upon which sat a curl of some sort of sausage with an orange/yellow skin, and pale, meaty innards. Altogether, I guessed, the sausage section — for it had been cut from a larger length of sausage — was about twenty centimetres long. Eva divided the sausage into three and invited me to help myself to the green vegetable. I took a small portion at first and we tucked into our sausage which I found to be quite tasty. The greens, however, were very bitter but I tried valiantly to eat the portion I had taken. I asked what it was. Daan had difficulty finding the English word, suggesting at first that it was spinach, but I noted that it was far more bitter than that. It was a mystery and remained so, as far as I was concerned, for many years. It was, of course, kale, that much-loved discovery of the healthy brigade in recent years. Remember how much of the stuff had been on offer in that large pot! And there was no alternative or escape. Sausage, kale and more kale. Naturally, I was as polite as I could be about dinner, but I did struggle. I have completely forgotten what we had for dessert, such is the imprint of that main course. My lecture the following morning was politely received as nobody in that department worked in any area close to mine. I shouldn't have gone there really, but I had followed advice from an acquaintance in Amsterdam.

I left Nijmegen early in the afternoon for Leiden, and another university I had not visited before. Leiden University is very old and one of the grand universities of Europe. I had been booked into a hotel in the old part of the city, getting there by cab from the station. I wasn't due to meet my new host until the following morning. The hotel was as old as that part of Leiden in which it was situated.

As a rule, I prefer the anonymity of plastic furniture, the boring sameness of the TV, the tea-making jug, the ensuite of the international motel, simply because of their reliability and guaranteed level of comfort. The hotel in which I was now billeted in Leiden could not have been more different. At first, my heart sank a notch as I carried my luggage up two floors and along a narrow, twisting corridor whose floor undulated far more even than that in Gwyn's and my seventeenth century cottage back home. It was rather like riding waves. The floor was little better in my bedroom which was, however, spacious and exquisitely interesting. Black oak panelling everywhere came complete with dust. The whole thing was as authentic as you could wish for. My bedside table and bureau were free of dust, mind, and the bed was made up with appetisingly clean linen.

I decided to eat in that evening for I had noticed a small dining room as I had entered the hotel which could have passed muster for that in many a fine English pub. I was curious to find out what sort of menu the place might offer. It turned out to be short but with several dishes to tempt international and local patrons alike and I chose a braise without regret; and a good bottle of red to wash it down. I moved through to another area afterwards to enjoy a good smoke of my pipe; another thing I had been obliged to forswear for some days.

When bedtime came round, I mounted the stairs, climbed two storeys and sailed along the narrow and twisting corridors to my room. I found that someone had placed a lovely hot stoneware water bottle in my bed. It had done its job, so I removed it before climbing up to get in. I say "climbed up" deliberately. The bed was really quite high and the mattress was one of those featherbed things on lax springs, the like of which I hadn't experienced since sharing my grandmother's bed when I was about five years old. At first, the lack of support was disconcerting but then the sheer sensuality of the setup overcame me. Surely, I thought, this is how the phrase "as snug as a bug in a rug" came to be coined. My pillow was equally soft — something I do not ordinarily like at all — but it all came together to give me the best experience in bed I have ever had on my own. I slept like a log that night in Leiden.

After a typical Dutch breakfast of cheese and ham, to which I had already grown quite partial after a couple of trips to Amsterdam, I was picked up by a post-doc member of my host's research team. There followed the usual meeting with my host's group, chatting about their work, a brief tour of the laboratories, which were brand new at that time, and so to my lecture.

This went very well. I was gratified with the level of interest and the number of questions, and at the end of the whole thing, my distinguished host, Jan Reedijk, who was head of the department as well as being someone whose work I had heard of several times before, presented me with a small medal by way of welcome. It was just a friendly gesture, a way of commemorating the fact that I was the first visiting speaker in that new building. It was a little joke really, but everyone, including me, rather enjoyed the ceremony. Afterwards, Jan and a few of his research group took me to the cafeteria for a spot of lunch. I was left to my own devices in Leiden for the afternoon, but arrangements were made for me to be picked up later and be taken for dinner. I filled my time with another of my random walks, ending up at one stage near the ever-present waterways of that lovely city.

At six o'clock, Jan drove up to my hotel with his wife, Ada. I spent some time getting acquainted with Ada, talking a little of Holland's architecture and of its beautiful tulip fields. Jan rather brusquely interrupted us after a very few minutes, and looking at his watch, announced that we only had exactly thirteen minutes left to get to the restaurant, whereupon he whisked everyone off to a restaurant he obviously thought very highly of. And it was, indeed, extremely good, for Jan had ordered a degustation dinner of nine courses, served with different wines for each. It was the first time that I had experienced such a thing and I was more than a little impressed.

During our meal, I mentioned my hotel and that while my normal preference was for the blandness and dependability of an international motel, I was more than delighted with the place I was in. Jan explained that he had chosen that hotel deliberately because he felt that I might enjoy a taste of the old. It really was a most enjoyable evening and when I felt relaxed enough to say it, I mentioned Jan's urgency in hurrying my conversation with Ada outside the hotel and his insistence that we had only thirteen minutes to get here. Surely a restaurant isn't bothered to that extent, I suggested. Ada smiled and told me that Jan was always like that.

'I don't like surprises,' Jan confessed.

By the sound of it, I thought, he had raised that thought to the level of a fetish. The conversation continued along these lines for some minutes until Ada herself used the word "fetish". We all laughed about it, but Jan insisted that he would continue to run his life by the clock. So that was that. In due course, they returned me to my hotel, and I was effusive in my thanks for their hospitality. I went upstairs and back to my burrow.

Next morning, as I was finishing my breakfast, I watched a substantial lady carry a large canvas bag and plonk it on an unoccupied table. I could have said "placed" but the fact is that she plonked it. All the tables in the foyer — for want of a better description — which served as a breakfast room also, were covered with large oriental rugs in sombre colours. Not cloth printed that way, but genuine rugs so stiff that they stuck well out beyond the wooden table tops they adorned. It was rather odd, I thought, but quite functional. This bag lady was dressed in a thick tweed, mustard-brown suit, with a double-breasted jacket over a straight skirt. She wore socks and very sensible shoes with leather tassels. Her hair was brushed back in a somewhat severe style and held in place by something I couldn't quite see. Without any apparent sign —

to me at any rate — patrons of the hotel went up to this lady and the large books which she had taken from her bag, to pay for their accommodation and whatnot. She wrote out a small receipt by hand and then waited for her next customer. It really was an interesting way to dispense with an office. I had no need to go up to see mother, however, as my room and meals were paid for by Jan's university. So I sloped off, caught a cab and train to Amsterdam airport, Schiphol, from where I flew to Stansted airport to be met by Gwyn, whom I regaled with tales of a long and thought-provoking tour.

Part III

10

In early 1991, I decided to make another foray into Germany. I had agreed to examine a candidate there for his doctorate. The hard work for this, of course, was done in Cambridge where I carefully read the thesis. I had been assured on the phone by the candidate's supervisor that everything should be straightforward. I wouldn't have agreed to do the job otherwise and I knew the supervisor by reputation as someone to be trusted on a thing like that.

The German system of PhD examinations is much like that in Britain and the States, with an internal and external examiner who examine the candidate in person afterwards in order to satisfy themselves that the thesis has been written by the candidate himself. I was perfectly satisfied with the candidate's written work and confidently expected the oral examination to go smoothly. I knew neither the candidate's supervisor nor the internal examiner personally on this occasion.

I was intrigued to make this trip to the Goethe University in Frankfurt. It is very new by Cambridge standards, having been founded in 1918 — although, actually, there are roots going back to the fifteenth century — as the Universität

Frankfurt am Main but renamed in 1932 in honour of von Goethe, probably the best known of Frankfurt's famous sons. Twenty Nobel Laureates have been associated with this new university, a remarkable fact, Max von Laue, physicist in crystal diffraction; Max Born, Hans Bethe and Otto Stern, all quantum physicists; being some with connection to my areas of endeavour. None of that is really relevant, of course, but I have always argued that there might be something in the air which I could inhale...

There is nothing special to report about the examination, in which the candidate was perfectly competent and was awarded his doctorate in due course, or, for that matter, about my brief stay in Frankfurt. I had flown in from Stansted and would return the same way, but I felt it would be nice to include three other visits while I was over in Germany. Geographically, they fall into an almost straight line. A loop might have been better, but I accepted being a shuttlecock on this occasion.

I planned to visit Dirk Reinen in Marburg, George Sheldrick in Göttingen, and Werner Urland in Hanover. I had never met Reinen but had become acquainted with his work, which was very much in my own area, through a colleague in Tasmania who had worked with him intermittently and who admired him greatly. Sheldrick had been a colleague of mine in Cambridge, and Urland had been a doctoral student with me at University College in London. All in all, I was looking forward to this tour.

I planned to stay in Marburg for just one night. After a short rail journey from Frankfurt, I arrived in Marburg in time for lunch with a member of Reinen's research group in the university cafeteria, after which there was a brief tour of the chemical laboratories at the Philipps-Universität before giving my lecture at four o'clock. There was some sharp questioning about my ideas after the lecture which went on for some time. After a while Reinen himself stopped the formal proceedings and asked me if we might continue these discussions within his research group tomorrow. I explained that I would be leaving for my next port of call early in the morning. Reinen was very disappointed, not having realised what arrangements had been made. Indeed, in view of the obvious interest in his subject, I was disappointed too and wished that I'd allocated more time in Marburg; and I said so.

Reinen thought for a moment and then asked if I would be willing to come back into the lab at six-thirty p.m. to have informal discussions with him and his group. He explained that he would have me taken to my hotel now, have me brought back a little later, and after the meeting, some of his students would take me for dinner. I was only too happy to oblige and so it happened.

There were about half a dozen people in Dirk Reinen's office when I arrived. Dirk himself, a couple of post-doctoral Fellows or senior, I guessed, and three or four postgraduate students. Several things soon became abundantly clear to me, that everyone in the room was intensely interested in what I had to say, they knew a lot about my work already, and that the professor was undoubtedly the boss. He was charming, most attentive and polite but what he said, went. They asked so many questions and I really enjoyed answering them.

There was no question of anyone trying to upstage anyone else. It was a meeting of genuinely interested scientists like nothing I had experienced before outside my own group. Reinen was a fair-haired man, slight of build but upright and authoritative. He was genuinely charming in his hospitality and regretted not having realised how short my visit would be. In appearance at least, he reminded me of my own father.

At one point, Dirk looked at his watch and brought the meeting to an abrupt halt. It was eight o'clock and nobody had seemed to notice time passing. There were many thankyous all round and I was whisked away by one of the post docs and one of the postgrads for dinner in town. It was dark outside by this time and we made our way out of the university campus on foot, over the main railway tracks, and quite near the rail station itself, up to the face of a low cliff which I had vaguely noticed upon my arrival in the town that morning.

My hosts explained that we would eat at a restaurant in the old part of the town and indicated a door in the wall of the cliff before which they were standing. I wondered what sort of place we were going to, some sort of rabbit's burrow, maybe? The door was simply that of a lift however, a modern lift, which elevated us by maybe thirty metres. We stepped out into the middle of the old town. The contrast with the modern railway station down below at the bottom of the cliff as well as the new buildings of the university could not have been more acute. It was like stepping back three centuries. I couldn't see very much in the dark of night but did glimpse old timbered and stone buildings pleasantly lit by tasteful lamps around the place. Sadly, it had begun to drizzle so we hurried along to get into the warmth and dry of their chosen eating place.

It was a cosy restaurant, and we all enjoyed a leisurely meal, chatting about chemists in Düsseldorf, politics in Germany and around the world, and almost anything. I ate a steak served with baked potato and sauerkraut. Not subtle, maybe, but very well cooked and I enjoyed it. After a beer or two and all my concentration of the past few hours, I began to feel decidedly sleepy. My hosts took me back to my hotel where I slept like a baby. At breakfast next morning, I again regretted not having allocated more time to these folk in Marburg but yet was pleased and confident that I had given a good account of myself and that my hosts had understood my propositions. I left Marburg in a happy frame of mind.

After a few hours on the train, I arrived in Göttingen and was met by George Sheldrick. I hadn't planned to lecture there. Instead, this was just to be a brief overnight stop to see a former colleague. George Sheldrick was a very clever chap indeed who had been a lecturer in Cambridge when I arrived with Johnson and Lewis from University College, London. He had recently moved into crystallography; a subject I had equally recently left. I had worked in two areas for my PhD at Imperial College, several years earlier, crystallography and magnetochemistry. In 1940, say, the solving of one crystal structure would be sufficient for someone's doctorate simply because such analyses require some heavy numerical computation. In the forties, for example, there were no such things as computers and the work had to be done by hand.

Many tricks were developed to help in that process, but the fact remains that it could take two or three years to complete these calculations and solve the crystal structure of just one quite simple substance.

By the time that I entered the field in the early sixties as a graduate student of Ronald Mason, computers were being exploited by many research groups. The calculations were the same, but a result could be achieved in a few months or less, instead of years. A PhD thesis in chemical crystallography, then, might describe studies of six or ten molecules, depending upon their complexity.

It was already clear to me, as I finished my doctoral thesis, that the whole business was on the verge of being automated. I therefore turned my attention to my other pursuits — magnetochemistry and ligand-field theory, which are closely related to one another.

George, however, had just moved into crystallography as I remarked above. At first, I had thought that George had made a mistake for, as just noted, the field was fast becoming a technology rather than a science in my opinion. However, it soon became apparent that George was writing computer programs to tackle *every* aspect of solving crystal structures. He was, in effect, becoming *the* automator, if that is a word (and if it isn't, it should be), of the discipline himself. By the time that George had left Cambridge to take up a chair in Göttingen, he was well on the way to world renown as such.

I mused about George during my train journey from Marburg, recalling two amusing events in George's life. They were really two examples of the same thing, one being from my own memory and the other from Gwyn's. George was undoubtedly a bright man in his field but was less smart in matters of simple, ordinary life. I recalled seeing him from my car window one day. George was walking along on a drizzly day with his very young firstborn held over his shoulder and pointing backwards. George was being a good dad and bouncing the baby as he strode along. Unknown to George, the baby was spewing vomit all over the back of George's woollen jumper as they made their way.

Gwyn's memory was of seeing George pushing the bairn in a low pushchair against a howling gale of wind and rain. The child was howling fit to bust. George stopped and said to his baby, 'Now just tell Daddy *exactly* what the matter is…' The howls continued unabated. I have noted several times throughout life's journey, this coupling of academic brilliance with quotidian gaucherie. As a friend of ours has often observed in similar circumstances, 'More degrees than a thermometer but no common sense.'

After greeting me at Göttingen station, George drove me to his home where we settled down for drinks and a chat. It had been the first time, really, that we two had had a heart-to-heart. During our conversation, I asked George why he had chosen to leave Cambridge for Göttingen, readily admitting, however, that Göttingen was Germany's oldest university and a most prestigious one at that. Interestingly enough, it had been founded in 1734 by King George II of Great Britain, *and Elector of Hanover*! It is the oldest university in the state of Lower Saxony and today claims some forty-four Nobel Prize winners. George pointed out that he had a brother living in Germany, that he had been a regular visitor and that he spoke the language fluently, and that he liked the place, all of which aligned to support his move. Apart from that, in those days, promotion in Cambridge was a very slow business. It was to be several years more before I made reader and there was absolutely no chance of becoming a full professor. The system wasn't constructed like that. Things were different in most other universities in Britain but that isn't the point. It was common to find that academics who eventually left Cambridge (or Oxford, for that matter) would walk straight into a chair somewhere else. Nor is it the point when I note that the promotional structure in Cambridge today is vastly different from what it was then.

Anyway, George wanted that position, he was offered a marvellous opportunity in Göttingen in a country he knew and loved; a position, furthermore, which came with more than adequate funding for his research; so he took it. I couldn't blame him. George's computer programs have become *de rigueur* in crystallographic circles and rightly so.

It was good to catch up. I left the following morning for Hanover through which I had passed, or rather at where I had changed trains, on my earlier journeys to Braunschweig. This time, Hanover itself was my destination. My former student, Werner Urland, met me himself. Werner was by now a professor at the Leibnitz University of Hanover.

Werner had been a postgraduate student of mine many years earlier and I remembered his traumatic introduction to life in Britain. He had had his pocket picked while travelling on the tube on his first day at University College, losing some fifty quid, as far as I can recall. Maybe it was more. The point is that he was left without means to pay his rent for the month, let alone his food and he was, quite naturally, pretty upset. Our professor, none other than Jack Lewis, with whom I later moved to Cambridge, turned up trumps and raided a small slush fund he controlled as professor, from which he reimbursed Werner for his loss. That was splendid, but the experience had been a rotten one for Werner, nonetheless.

Werner had been a first-rate research student, had worked hard and produced a lot of good work. He was an asset to my group in other ways also for he joined in all the social — or sometimes antisocial — activities of my group members. He was "one of the boys" and learned from, and taught, his fellows about some pretty heavy drinking so far as I was able to discern.

Several years later, I met Werner once more, for he had come to Cambridge to join David Buckingham, the professor of theoretical chemistry there, as a post doc wanting to go far deeper into theory than I was able to teach. But we socialised together on several occasions. Now it was Werner's turn to be host when I gave my lecture in Hanover. Werner had booked me into an hotel near the centre of Hanover for a couple of nights, and left me there for the first evening, having made arrangements for a busy day following.

He picked me up next morning and took me off to the laboratories at the university where, as had become usual on these trips, I had conversations with some of Werner's research students, took a brief tour of the labs and was conducted to the lecture theatre where I was to sing my song.

There was fair interest in what I had to say, and I was happy enough with the range and number of questions which followed. People were leaving the lecture theatre at the end while I was collecting together my notes and slides, when a young man came up to me, and in a very thick German accent, congratulated me on my English. Several other students around made agreeing noises.

'But I *am* English!' I protested.

'Ah yes,' came the reply, 'but we have many lecturers from Japan and other Asian countries who lecture in English and we can't understand a word they say.'

I treasure that interaction, quite hilarious.

After that, I was taken off for a pleasant lunch by several of the research students who questioned me about Cambridge — a topic which regularly comes up under these circumstances — until I was taken to Werner's office. We spent quite some time reminiscing about London and Cambridge until Werner suggested that he take me for a drive around Hanover on our way to his home. I saw Hanover as a lively place with lots of signs of happy activity everywhere.

I met Werner's wife later who cooked a splendid meal for the three of us. She was a fun sort of person with a whimsical turn of mind which I enjoyed. Eventually, Werner drove me back to my hotel for my last night in a city I was beginning to warm to.

11

There followed the train journey from Hanover to Frankfurt, this time not through Marburg which does not lie on the main line. Further, the train was one of Germany's ICE trains, very common these days but less so in 1991. There was a speed indicator in prime position at the end of each carriage. When I inspected it, I found that we were travelling at around 298 kilometres per hour. The ride was so stable, I could barely believe it. I felt that the train was floating. It was an altogether delightful experience; the buffet was very nicely organised, and snacks were also on offer as waiters came round from time to time. I reckon that high-speed trains are a far better experience than flying.

    I didn't read a book — I rarely did in those days, as I have repeatedly told you — but settled down to a quiet recollection of my week or so in Germany. I knew my talks in Marburg and Hanover had gone well; you can tell these things. I had been amazed by the grilling — though that is too confrontational a word in the circumstances — I had received in Marburg at the hands of the steely-eyed boss-man, Dirk Reinen, but had been more than gratified by the interest and courtesy he had shown. Then there was that hilarious compliment from the German host in Hanover about my English. It all went to make for a happy and fulfilling trip. So different, I felt, from my time in Germany on the previous two occasions.

This time, I looked upon the Germans I had met in much the same way as the French, the Spaniards, the Italians, the Dutch, or the Swiss. All different, both as national groups and as individuals, but all interesting people with whom I could get along swimmingly. So what had been the matter in Germany before? Again, I rehearsed my fears of spies from the GDR, or of continuing antagonism on my part towards my country's enemy when I was a kid, or of the Holocaust. But had those concerns disappeared suddenly, just because I had met some people who liked my work? Could be. Of course, one glaring difference between this trip and those earlier was that Braunschweig had not been on my itinerary this time. More to the point, East Germany wasn't in the mix.

I might interject here, dear reader, and remind you that all this anguish was taking place in 1991, and not today after German reunification and much wealth sharing has achieved so much in the new, greater Germany.

In addition to the anger which I had felt when I saw what obscenities had been done to the purely physical environment in the East, I had also been overcome by an intense depression on seeing the poverty of the place. And that had been compounded by a sense of guilt when I thought that there might be some justice in that suffering because of Germany having started the war. And then by a further layer of guilt when I remembered that all wars have right and wrong on both or all sides, in this case, not least by the stupidity of the "winner" in the Great War. In general, I believe, almost all the suffering of ordinary people has been at the hands of greedy, selfish, arrogant minorities who believed that the world should be theirs and who were prepared to go to indescribable lengths at everyone else's expense to get it. Then again, many ordinary people who got involved in wars, did things they wouldn't ordinarily contemplate, simply because they had to. Like countless people before and after me, I soon sank into a soup of confusion and dense mental mist. However, just because one is unable to get a grip on the logic of a situation does not diminish the intensity of one's feelings. It's all very well for folk to decry my thoughts as xenophobic — and I was very concerned lest they indeed were — but at least, I was trying to work out what my problem was. Making fun of the way people pronounced my own language wasn't xenophobia. It mightn't be very clever, but I didn't believe that to be serious. I knew, of course, of people who could and would preach about any little thing which might cause offence to others, but I argued, it is part of life; we all get the rough end of something and it might just be better to suck it up; in short, to grow up.

But right now, I was far more concerned about something which I felt was much bigger than such peccadillos. But what was it? Surely, I thought, the depression I felt in the East, maybe just being confronted by a level of poverty which, though hardly devastating by world standards, was more than I had previously encountered, had upset me so. I had always recoiled from scenes of depression conveyed in films or in literature (what little I had read at that time). I remembered when my father, who had no particular skills to offer, cried when he lost his job when I was about eleven years old, had tried several others which had lasted only weeks, and finally quit this one because it was too demeaning and duplicitous, and so poorly paid. I remembered the sudden panic in the family about how we were going to live, to eat. Well, Dad got another job within three weeks and it was one he liked well enough to hang onto for the rest of his working life but at the time, nothing could be seen on the horizon. I never forgot that scene, that desolation and helplessness.

That was long ago, of course, and my mum and dad were happy enough afterwards, but was my horror of poverty rooted in that time? Certainly, seeing similar scenes acted out in films, evoked very strong feelings in me. I'm afraid that they put me off reading some of D. H. Lawrence's books — not his poetry, though — or those of John Steinbeck, for example. I'm not sure whether I have got too far along with Lawrence's works even today. So, I decided after some hours of admittedly lazy thinking, that my experiences of the Fence, and later, of the GDR had been responsible for my discomfort with, and on the second trip especially, my fear of Germany as a whole. But I wasn't sure. I never come quickly to conclusions on matters as important as this.

In due course, I arrived in Frankfurt and its airport and found my way past customs in the direction of the departure lounge for my flight home to Stansted. I was an hour and a bit early, so I found myself an armchair in a nearby bar and indulged in a double whisky. While sitting there, I looked up at the distant departure board to check that my flight was registered. It was but was slated as one hour delayed. I was annoyed for I knew that Gwyn, who was going to meet me at Stansted, would have left home by now because she always left a lot of time when dealing with airports. This was in those days before mobile phones (at least for ordinary mortals) so there was no way of letting her know the problem; she was going to be hanging around at Stansted for a couple of hours. There was nothing I could do about it.

In due course, there came an announcement explaining the problem. Apparently, the aircraft which was to have flown me to Stansted had been delayed because of technical problems. Later on, further bulletins clarified the matter — or reluctantly became honest, if you want my jaundiced opinion — and explained that the plane hadn't even left Stansted because of those technical problems so that I would have to join the next flight from Frankfurt to Stansted which would be on a plane which had only just left Stansted. Later came an announcement which admitted that that plane was still on the ground at Stansted. In the end, I left Frankfurt four hours after I was due to and Gwyn had to hang around at Stansted for nearly five hours altogether. Well, such things are not unheard of, of course, and I mention it because of events which occurred at Frankfurt airport while I was keeping a few glasses of scotch company.

I was seated near, but not actually at, the bar which was a circular affair in the middle of that part of the large, carpeted lounge. It had several bar stools fixed around it but only one customer was seated, apart from me in my chair nearby. There came a small party — probably four but I cannot be sure now — of Arabs wearing their traditional headdress of kufiyah with agal, together with western-style suits. I was unable to comment on the quality of the kufiyah, although they looked very neat, but I was aware immediately of the high quality of their suits. They were very, very expensive. Two of the Arabs were smoking large cigars. All of them were rather excited and very loud.

I have never liked people speaking loudly, almost shouting in this instance, and especially rich people behaving like that. Maybe it's my English reticence. I think, however, that it's just a matter of good manners. The Arabs continued in this fashion as they sat down at the bar and began ordering champagne by the bottles, that's right, *bottles*. I attempted to ignore these spoilt arrivistes — New Richards, as a friend of Gwyn's and mine used to call them — but their noise made that impossible. One of them looked over in my direction, waved his arm theatrically and shouted at me to come and have a drink. I pointed at the whisky in my other hand, but they insisted, saying that I must join them so that they could say thank you.

'What for?' I asked but that, of course, hooked me in. I walked over to the bar and sat down on a stool.

'For what you are doing in Kuwait,' the man replied. Then I remembered. As I was leaving for my trip round Germany, the Gulf War had just begun. A "Coalition of the Willing" had been formed by President Bush Sr. and forces were rapidly heading into Kuwait — and anticipated great danger — by the time I left home.

'Nothing to do with me,' I replied. 'I'm not the guy who did it.'

'Yes, you did,' the Arab insisted. 'You, the Americans, everybody; and we Kuwaitis are very grateful.'

On the face of it, that was a nice thing to do; to offer drinks to countrymen of those nations who had forces in danger — for that is very much how it seemed at the beginning of the Gulf War — fighting for theirs. And with the passing of time, maybe I should have seen it that way. But I didn't at the time. Firstly, I recognised that I had almost certainly made a mistake in thinking of these men as parvenues, nouveau riche; their money was likely two or three generations in the making. Secondly, these guys weren't representative of the average Arab or even the average Kuwaiti. These oil men, for that is what I now recognised them to be, were members of the privileged few who had persuaded the US and the world to come to their personal aid. Sure, Saddam Hussain was a bastard, but he had been the American's bastard till politicians made mistakes. As ever, the hypocrisy in all these things is unending.

It is doubtful that many of these thoughts were in my mind that day. It is far more likely that I simply saw over-privileged, loud-mouthed yobs attempting to corral me into their group. I accepted one glass of their champagne but when they tried to give me more, I found the spine to refuse. I did it as politely as I could, saying that I had an important meeting to attend and that I needed to keep a clear head, but thank you anyway, etcetera… I managed to extricate myself and go back to my armchair.

I took out a folder from my briefcase in an effort to look busy and realised that all this nonsense had, at least, provided some distraction to while away my long wait. My flight was called eventually, and in due course, I found myself in a snake of disembarked passengers making our way past the final barrier to the main concourse at Stansted. I hoped that Gwyn would be somewhere on the other side of the screen waiting for me. Gwyn and I were cat lovers, are cat lovers, cat adorers. We frequently communicate with each other with a "mau" when proper words aren't really necessary. As my queue ever so slowly neared the exit, I called out into the air, loud and clear, 'Mau.' There was an immediate reply in like kind from the other side of the screen. Gwyn was there; pissed off for the long wait we had both endured, but there.

After

12

It was in April, probably a year or so later that I received a letter from Rudolf Krause saying that he and Greta planned to visit Britain in June for a touring holiday, that he'd like to pop into Cambridge, and that he would appreciate my showing Greta something of my college. I was only too happy to oblige, and indeed, it was a marvellous opportunity for me to return the hospitality the Krauses had shown me in Braunschweig. Gwyn was curious to meet the wife of the man she remembered as a hypochondriac. I suggested that the Krauses come for an extended weekend and it was so arranged.

Greta and Gwyn got on very well together. They seemed to laugh at the same things, but more to the point, they laughed. Rudolf, however, was his usual measured self. Most polite and grateful for everything Gwyn and I did for them — a long trek round some of Cambridge's famous colleges, lunch at high table in my own college, dinners at home, courtesy of Gwyn, and a short drive around some of the neighbouring villages — but he was dour, as ever. Once more, Gwyn was forcibly struck with his hypochondria. He would talk endlessly about slight ailments and of how he treated them. Greta looked somewhat embarrassed as he droned on.

At one point, and I can't quite remember how it came up, the conversation turned to trains. Rudolf almost became excited then, babbling on about railway timetables, including those for the local services in Cambridgeshire.

On the third morning of their stay, Gwyn suggested that we make a trip to Wisbech where she wanted to buy some samphire, a delicacy of which she and I are inordinately fond, and it was the right time of year for it. Rudolf had heard of Wisbech from his railway manuals and thought it would be a good thing to do. Greta was happy simply to be taken out for the morning, so off we went. As we approached the town, both Gwyn and Greta noticed some small notices on boards stuck into the grass verge by the side of the road. They advertised a model railway exhibition in the town somewhere. Greta looked at Gwyn; Gwyn looked at Greta. Neither spoke. Neither I nor Rudolf saw the signs and Greta grinned at Gwyn as I drove on into town. Greta really enjoyed the little farmers' market in Wisbech, and Gwyn found her samphire.

After our guests had departed to explore other parts of Britain, Gwyn and I both breathed a sigh of relief. Not for Greta's departure but certainly for Rudolf's. I felt guilty at feeling that way for, on the face of it, Rudolf had been an exemplary guest. That was part of the problem in a way. One could go on and on about how polite and courteous he was. Remembering his generosity of spirit when purchasing groceries at that little shop in the newly freed East Germany, of how long he had spent just chatting to the shop-owner. Rudolf was a kind man; of that there was no doubt. The simple truth was, however, that he was a *crashing bore*. Whenever we had met, I had felt terribly constrained — permanently on edge, if you like — by my desire to be a polite guest.

The more I thought about that simple conclusion, the more I began to think that all that stuff I had felt about Germany on my first two trips — those which had included Braunschweig and Krause — should be laid at Krause's, all too kindly, door. My earlier conclusion was that it was the depressing sights of what the GDR had done to the people of the East which had been responsible for my ennui on those occasions. That it had been far more than ennui, that it had grown to fear, was surely my own fault, I believed. But by this time, memory was fading a little and I couldn't be sure.

But I had come to realise that I had made such a silly mistake.